TQC Wisdom of Japan
Managing for Total Quality Control

TQC Wisdom of Japan
Managing for Total Quality Control

Hajime Karatsu
Translated by David J. Lu

Foreword by
Norman Bodek, President
Productivity, Inc.

Originally published by
JUSE Press Ltd., Tokyo

Productivity Press
Cambridge, MA
Norwalk, CT

Originally published as *TQC Nihon no chie*
by Hajime Karatsu, copyright © 1981 by
JUSE Press, Ltd. (Tokyo)

English translation rights arranged with
JUSE Press, Ltd. through Japan Foreign-
Rights Centre.

English translation copyright © 1988 by
Productivity Press, Inc.

PO 1348·

Productivity Press
P.O. Box 3007
Cambridge, MA 02140
(617) 497-5146

Library of Congress Catalog Card Number: 87-062302
ISBN: 0-915299-18-6

Cover design: Russ Funkhouser
Typeset by Rudra Press, Cambridge, MA
Printed and bound by The Maple-Vail Book Manufacturing Group
Printed in the United States of America

Library of Congress Cataloging-in-Publication Data

Karatsu, Hajime, 1919-
  TQC Wisdom of Japan

    Translation of: *TQC Nihon no chie*.
    Includes index.
    1. Quality control — Japan.   2. Production management — Japan.   I. Title.
TS155.K3313   1988   658.5'62'0952   87-62302
ISBN 0-915299-18-6

88 89 90 91   10 9 8 7 6 5 4 3 2 1

Contents

Publisher's Foreword

Deming Prize winner Hajime Karatsu is one of Japan's best known quality experts and also one of its most controversial spokesmen. Long associated with Matsushita, both as a managing director and special advisor, Karatsu has also consulted with many other leading Japanese corporations. He is a faculty member at Tokai University's Research and Development Institute and a member of the fifth generation computer committee for the government of Japan. With other members of that committee, Hajime Karatsu is looking towards the twenty-first century to identify new opportunities for industry. An outspoken critic of U.S. industrial management and international trade policies, Karatsu recently participated in a series of panel discussions published in the *New York Times* on Japan-U.S. relations.

Karatsu doesn't hold his punches. He is direct and open, occasionally challenging, but always forthright in his opinions. He berates U.S. CEOs who consistently focus on short-term profits, and are more interested in stock price gains than in the real growth to be achieved through increased productivity and quality in the company's products and services.

In the battle for world markets, quality separates the winners and the losers — and U.S. companies are losing, because lower quality makes American products more costly. Many American firms continue to transplant their manufacturing operations to the Far East to reduce costs, in spite of the fact — clearly shown in this book — that better management and improved quality would more than compensate for the dollar differences that concern those companies now.

It is ironic to see American companies going to the Far East to take advantage of lower labor costs, while Japanese and Korean manufacturers are coming to the United States for the same reason. How can they produce more economically in our country than we can? The difference is management know-how, understanding, and total commitment to quality. In the past we assumed that quality had to cost from ten to thirty percent of sales; now we are learning that these costs can be reduced tremendously through total quality control.

Total quality control (TQC) is a process and an awareness that world-class status is obtained only when everyone — every worker, manager, and executive — is completely responsible for the quality of the company's products and services. At one time, TQC was only a vision of how a world-class company should be run; now it is a reality in many leading Japanese corporations.

Today, U.S. companies have fewer and fewer options, and the world has become too small to protect us from our own mediocrity. With satellite technologies and jet transportation, our products compete with products from around the world. To become world-class manufacturers, we *must* produce only quality products and deliver only the highest quality services.

Karatsu believes that U.S industry can duplicate the Japanese quality success story. To succeed, says Karatsu, you must be as committed to quality as you are to the company's profit margin, and you must understand that in the end these two goals are inseparable.

This clear and simply written book can be viewed as an extended essay introducing the basic philosophy of TQC to senior management. A best-seller in Japan, where every worker expects to be involved in the quality effort, this book also serves as a valuable resource text for the quality expert. It offers a simple and compelling rationale for companywide involvement and places statistical process control in its proper context — as a tool to support the quality effort, not as an end in itself.

You'll find this book easy to read. But it's your job to get others to start following this practical advice — your CEOs, vice presidents, managers, quality managers, engineers, anyone concerned about quality and your company's survival.

We are proud to be able to bring this book to the attention of American readers. We are particularly grateful to Professor David Lu of Bucknell University for translating the book and helping to arrange for its publication in America. Our thanks also to the staff at JUSE Press, Ltd. in Tokyo for patiently answering our many questions and updating some of the factual information in the book. And finally, a special thanks to editors Connie Dyer and Camilla England, to our hard-working production manager, Esmé McTighe, and to the superb production staff at Rudra Press.

Norman Bodek
President, Productivity, Inc.

TQC Wisdom of Japan
Managing for Total Quality Control

CHAPTER 1

Prologue

Third Industrial Revolution

In 1980, Japan's auto industry produced 11 million units, surpassing the United States which, until then, had been the unchallenged master of the industry. This was a significant event that will be recorded in the chronicles of world industry. Rich in land and natural resources, the United States was a natural to become the first country to mass-produce automobiles. Now, however, it has lost its preeminence as the largest producer.

Japan's example proves that success in industry is not a matter of favorable and measurable conditions but rather depends on the ingenuity and effort of industrial leaders. Human factors, in the final analysis, are decisive.

Japanese cars have succeeded because they provide high quality at a reasonable cost. They burn less fuel, do not break down, and have an attractive appearance. With these advantages, smaller Japanese-made cars can command the same price as full-sized American cars and still remain competitive. No matter how luxurious a car is, if it malfunctions on the highway, it is not much of a car — a fact American manufacturers seem to find difficult to comprehend.

When it became clear that American car manufacturers could not compete successfully against Japanese imports, Japan agreed to impose export quotas for cars shipped to the United

States. Many Americans, however, are not satisfied with this solution. They feel that the problems of American car manufacturers result from their failure to produce the kinds of cars consumers want, and that those companies, therefore, are getting what they deserve. Reducing the volume of Japanese imports, they reason, would only raise sticker prices even higher. This in turn would lead to a resurgence of inflation — giving American car manufacturers yet another reason to raise prices. In America, however, a good product will sell itself even if it is priced high. Thus, knowledgeable Americans say that the Japanese success proves industries can prosper if they consistently produce high-quality products.

Japan occupies 0.3 percent of the world's land surface and its population represents only 2.7 percent of the world's total. Yet, its GNP has grown to more than 11 percent of the world's total. There are many reasons for this success, and quality control has definitely been a key factor. The Industrial Revolution was sparked by the development of the steam engine; a second revolution grew out of Henry Ford's assembly line production; now, Japan is showing the world the way to a third industrial revolution — through the effective use of quality control.

U.S.-Japan Semiconductor Conference of 1980

In March 1980, I attended the U.S.-Japan Semiconductor Conference in Washington, D.C. The conference was held in Washington in an effort to convince the federal government that, contrary to public opinion, there was no "semiconductor issue."

Initially, the balance of trade in semiconductors had favored the United States, with Japan importing more semiconductors than it exported. When Japan developed the 16K RAM chip, however, American firms began to make large purchases from Japan. Within a short time Japan commanded 40 percent of the U.S. market because of its superior ability to make the kind of product this market demanded.

Japan was then criticized for "dumping," an argument that might sound persuasive to the uninformed. While critics admitted that Japanese-made semiconductors were of good quality, they suggested that this was so because Japanese firms were eager to control the American market and were therefore willing to ship only their best semiconductors to the U.S. Proponents of this argument assumed that these semiconductors were expensive. When they turned out to be quite cheap, the critics claimed that Japan was selling semiconductors to American firms without regard to cost — in other words, that Japan was guilty of "dumping."

On first thought, it seems reasonable that good products must cost more; however, anyone who has studied quality control knows that whenever defects are eliminated through quality control, costs go down. This makes sense, since the value of materials, labor, and equipment used in production is recouped in the form of saleable products. When there are many defects, machines must be adjusted constantly, materials must be replaced, and the equipment's utilization rate drops. When the rejection rate decreases, however, that same equipment's productive capacity increases greatly and cost drops significantly. In my presentation at the conference, I emphasized this point and insisted that the cost of Japanese semiconductors actually fell as the quality went up.

In my opening remarks to the conference, I noted that Japan, like the U.S., is a loser when inflation is high and that, at an 18 percent inflation rate, Japan loses $10 million a day on its foreign currency holdings. As the previous example illustrates, however, the best remedy for inflation is increased productivity. In the United States, productivity simply has refused to go up; Japan, by contrast, has succeeded in this area by the skillful application of quality control. Americans certainly know what quality control is — after all, the United States first taught Japan to use it. And so, I concluded my presentation by suggesting to my American friends that they return to the basics and aim at attaining higher quality.

My presentation was received very well. From that time on, the once fierce U.S. criticism of Japanese semiconductors was muted.

The Challenge of PPM

Mr. R. W. Anderson of Hewlett-Packard was the next speaker. He presented a comparison of U.S. and Japanese products in terms of quality indicators. The data were shocking enough to generate heated discussion.

Products from three Japanese companies were compared to products from three American companies. (See Table 1.) The data included defects discovered on delivery and after 1,000 hours of service. In terms of quality standards, Japanese products rated almost twice as high as those made by American manufacturers.

Manufacturer	Defective on Delivery	Failure after 1000 hours	Quality Evaluation
Japanese Co. I	0	0.01	89.9
Japanese Co. II	0	0.019	87.2
Japanese Co. III	0	0.012	87.2
American Co. I	0.19	0.09	86.1
American Co. II	0.11	0.059	63.3
American Co. III	0.19	0.267	48.1

Table 1. Comparison of Japanese and U.S. Semiconductors

While willing to concede *some* difference in quality, several of the American journalists present were not prepared to accept these figures because they indicated too sharp a difference. They interviewed different speakers, hoping to hear that there were no visible differences in quality. But in the end even these skeptics accepted the data.

The point made about quality in the semiconductor seminar was repeated again when I was a guest of the U.S. Department of Defense at its Very High Speed Integrated Circuit (VHSIC) project in March 1986.

At the beginning of my presentation, I showed a table of ac-celerated life test data. (See Table 2.)

In accelerated life tests conducted on 4000-series integrated circuits (IC) produced by all semiconductor manufacturers, dif-ferent batches of 100 sample chips from U.S. manufacturers were subjected to temperatures as high as 85 degrees Celsius and humidity reaching 85 percent. Interestingly, the chips broke down in different ways.

The first group of 100 ICs recorded no failures after testing for 1,000 to 5,000 hours. All 100 samples passed, even after with-standing 10,000 hours under the extreme conditions.

The second group of 100 sample chips did not fare as well. Two were discovered to be defective before testing began; 38 broke down after 2,000 hours; 39 more after 3,000 hours; and all 100 had failed after testing for 5,000 hours.

Another batch of 100 chips had no trouble up to 3,000 hours but in further testing they all broke down in a random pattern.

The manufacturing equipment used to produce these chips was generally about the same. The number of companies man-ufacturing and supplying the silicon wafers in the semiconductor manufacturing process was fixed, and the pattern designs were almost identical. Since we could not expect any major differ-ences in the capabilities of engineers, their work or workplaces, what was the reason for the differences noted in the accelerated life test? The answer again was quality control, and I cannot emphasize this point enough.

When quality control was first introduced to Japan, many false perceptions developed. Some people believed that while defects might be reduced significantly, they could not be elimi-nated completely as long as processes were controlled only statistically. But our actual performance proved this perception wrong. To measure defects, we relied first on percentages, in

Company	Sample Size	Hours									Defect	Defect / Sample
		240	504	1.000	2.000	3.000	4.000	5.000	6.000	7.000		
A	100	0	0	1	0	1	0	1	2	5	10	10 / 100
B	100	0	0	0	0	0	0	0	0	0	0	0 / 100
C	100	0	2	3	17	35	6	12	5	8	88	88 / 100
D	98	0	0	0	38	39	17	4	X	X	98	98 / 98
E	100	0	0	0	0	0	1	0	0	1	2	2 / 100
F	100	0	0	0	6	23	21	18	26	6	100	100 / 100

Test Condition: 85°C   85% RH   VDD-15V

Table 2. CMOS IC 4000 Series Accelerated Test

other words, so many defects per 100. Today, however, many plants measure in terms of PPM, that is, so many defects per million units.

The implication is clear. If we pursue quality control to eradicate the causes of defects one by one, defective units can be eliminated almost entirely. In today's complex systems built with tens of thousands of parts, unless quality assurance is based on PPM, the expanded potential for failure may render them useless.

Dr. W.A. Shewhart in the United States was the first to suggest applying concepts of statistical quality control to measure quality in terms of ever-decreasing rejection rates. But Japanese quality control has played a central role. At each workplace in Japan, everyone participates in a quality control (QC) circle aimed at making effective use of statistical quality control methods. Such a practice was not even dreamed of by the American founders of QC.

Adhere to Quality — Don't Blame Unions

The following story, featured in the June 6, 1986 *Business Week*, is one example of how U.S. management frequently fails to handle factors related to quality control successfully. In Fremont, California, there is a famous factory operated under a joint venture agreement between General Motors and Toyota. Before the establishment of the joint venture, GM had complete control of the plant, but management's relations with the United Auto Workers (UAW) turned sour. Strikes occurred frequently and the plant eventually closed down. Under the terms of the joint venture agreement, the UAW members were rehired when the plant reopened.

The new management was also worried about strikes and other labor-related problems. But no major problems arose, as management engaged in an intensive program of employee education. Today, productivity and product quality at the Fremont plant are almost equal to Toyota's plants in Japan — the joint venture has succeeded admirably.

The *Business Week* article provides an interesting insight into management practices. Union workers have been blamed for the poor quality of American-made cars, but the GM-Toyota joint venture proves otherwise. Managers frequently blame unions for the nation's ills; however, this is a mistake which tends only to highlight their own lack of commitment to quality.

CHAPTER 2

Quality Control and the Role of Top Management

The Boom in Total Quality Control

A t one time, talking about the Japanese people was a media "trend," both in Japan and elsewhere. Journalists were eager to discover some unique aspect of Japan and work it up into an article. With all this interest, it was strange that the quality control circle activities that were widely practiced and unique to Japanese companies were initially overlooked. I pointed this out in one of my article titled "The Workplace that Really Makes a Difference."

Today it is no secret that Japan's economic strength and industrial power are supported by widespread application of quality control procedures. A continuous flow of visitors from overseas passes through Japan's factories to observe, and many countries have requested QC instructors.

In the meantime, the mass media have suddenly begun to report on Total Quality Control (TQC), quality control, and the QC circle — and not just in journals that specialize in management and business. Even the national press, such as *Asahi*, *Mainichi*, and *Yomiuri*, now report on these issues almost daily, and recently the Japan Broadcasting Association (NHK) produced a Japanese version of the NBC special, "If Japan Can, Why Can't We?" I'm afraid the boom in media interest in QC throughout Japan is a direct result of its overseas reputation. In a way, QC has been "re-imported" to Japan.

It is often said that by the time the mass media decide to promote an issue, popular interest in it is probably declining. But in the case of the spread and wide acceptance of TQC, interest is growing as media coverage increases. Frankly, however, so much media attention is scarcely a blessing for companies committed to quality control. One auto manufacturer, reporting that as many as 130 teams from overseas had come to observe its plants, expressed concern that its real work could not progress with so many visitors.

Quality control was formally introduced to Japan in 1950, so we now have close to four decades of experience and accomplishments in the field. Initially, it was practiced exactly the way it was imported, but with improvement after improvement, Japanese QC acquired its own distinct style. The manufacturing sector was the first to practice QC, without regard to the state of the economy; now it is growing in the service sector. QC is continuing to grow in Japan, both qualitatively and quantitatively. No statistics show which Japanese companies practice QC — naturally, no company will admit it does not engage in quality control at all. There is, however, a system for registering QC circle activities with the QC Circle Headquarters. As of May 30, 1987, there were some 253,541 QC circles registered with it, with 2,039,094 members.

Not Cultural Differences

As more and more foreign teams travel to Japan to observe QC circles at work in our factories, they begin to find excuses for Japan's success. Some attribute it to the homogeneity of the Japanese as a nation and to their dedication to quality. Others point to lifetime employment provided by Japanese firms which engenders worker loyalty and, they claim, is the reason why the Japanese do not seek overtime pay and are happy to share their views on process improvement with management. They also state that Japanese unions do not object to QC. All in all, the situation is one many foreign firms envy.

Visitors to our factories are especially interested in QC circle activities, and their questions show this. Japanese plant managers give special attention to these questions, and so the topic of conversation inevitably turns to QC. A team of 20 managers from a European country recently visited a Matsushita plant. After a tour and briefing, the team asked to talk to the workers directly without management personnel present; they wanted to know what the workers' "true, unbiased feelings" were. We agreed and left them with two young female employees to respond to their questions. Later on, the two women reported that the visitors asked about wages, education and training, relationships with superiors, boyfriends — indeed, every imaginable topic. And the more these women told the visitors, the more the Europeans seem to have been impressed, although the women felt that "they were being exhibited like a pair of pandas."

From the European perspective, Japanese labor-management relations appear unique. Foreign observers tend to attribute this to cultural aspects peculiar to Japan. This theory is easy to understand and, in some quarters it is the accepted one. I do not wish to reject the theory out of hand, but those who consider culture the only factor in the Japanese success story overlook many other important features. When Japanese transistor radios flooded the world market, many people attributed this success to the manual dexterity of Japanese women workers. In general, people who ascribe economic performance to cultural features all make the same sort of superficial observation. They may be partly correct, but they never grasp the essentials.

It does not take much reflection to see why this is true. The United States and Europe are culturally quite different from Japan. Many American and European companies have excellent quality control, manufacture superb products and manage their affairs well. By the same token, there are many poorly managed companies in Japan, employing many presumably excellent and well paid workers, who hold jobs protected under the lifetime employment system. These companies are established and well known around the world. Yet they have poor employee morale, and their products do not enjoy good reputations. They operate in the red and barely survive. Year after year, some companies go bankrupt. And all of this happens in Japan. How can it be said that the Japanese economic success is based on culture? A Japanese company that relied on that sort of thinking would be courting disaster!

✳ Difference in Management Ability

If the superiority of Japanese products and Japanese economic performance is not due to culture, it must be due to some other factor. I believe the real answer lies in the abilities of Japanese management.

A company may have the very latest equipment and hardworking employees, but it cannot succeed if the management responsible for coordinating equipment and employees is ineffective. Many companies once plagued by infighting and lacking in capable top management have seen their fortunes change. They were rescued from economic difficulties by new management teams that overhauled the entire company. These teams understood that, ultimately, the quality of the people working in a company is not as important as their willingness to work. They also knew that workers' willingness to do their jobs is determined by the attitudes and abilities of their managers and brought the necessary qualities to their workplace.

Nowadays, some Japanese companies are moving their production facilities overseas. Journalists in Japan write frequently about manufacturers who have moved their plants to the United States, some emphasizing the risk of running afoul of the UAW. Other commentators speculate about the motives of Americans who want Japanese companies to establish facilities in their country. Perhaps, the argument runs, Americans hope to watch the Japanese fail right in their own backyard.

A Japanese manager visiting an American auto plant experiences the unexpected. It is another world compared to a Japanese plant. The engineer who guided me on one of my early visits seemed capable, and the plant appeared to be organizationally sound. The workplace, however, was another matter altogether: Workers smoked while working, and a veritable mountain of parts remained after components were assembled. A Japanese manager faced with such a situation would probably consider the plant unmanageable.

America is a big country, however, and other U.S. plants are very different from the one I've just described. I was especially impressed with a plant assembling jet aircraft engines and another producing computer parts for missiles. In the missile factory there were many alert and skillful women workers who had mastered precision work at the cutting edge of high technology and were proud of their work. In the jet engine factory the male workers wore neatly laundered white smocks and performed their tasks efficiently in a clean environment. It seemed that craftsmanship was alive and well in the United States.

It is important to keep in mind the leadership ability of whoever is at the helm. There will always be difficulties when Japanese companies move their factories to the United States. If top management is solid, however, there is nothing to fear.

The Freedom to Make Money and the Freedom to Go Bankrupt

When Kojin Ltd. (Textile Co. in Japan) went bankrupt, one national paper noted: "A company with a debt of ¥ 400 billion went bankrupt. Our economic system insists that we have the freedom to act, the freedom to make money, but also the freedom to go bankrupt. Thus the able firm wins and the inefficient one fails. It is a rapid process of natural selection and our process is quick."

These remarks capture the essence of our capitalist economy, which is the motivating force behind the growth of Japan's national economy.

Japanese manufacturers work hard to bring about improvement in their companies. Why? They fear that if they do not perform well, their company may go bankrupt and "lose the race." Anyone with experience in almost any sector of Japanese industry remembers the fierce competition in postwar Japan, which was excessive by any standard.

Industries have the freedom not to engage in quality control. That is a management decision. In our capitalist economy, however, there are also the freedom to fail in competition and the freedom to go bankrupt. Moreover, competition in quality is something everyone welcomes. A company that loses out in the cost and quality competition is not likely to get much sympathy.

Only 20 years ago, "made in Japan" was equivalent with cheap and defective products. But through our efforts at improving and controlling quality, "made in Japan" is now synonymous with the best products in the world. "Oh, this one is not as good as those made in Japan, but it functions quite well." These words, which an American friend of mine overheard in Paris when he bought a cigarette lighter, show how things have changed.

To what can we attribute this success? Although its land surface and population are small, Japan's economy (in terms of GNP) is now the second largest in the world.

Perhaps, one might think, Japan is blessed with many advantages. Geographically, however, Japan is far removed from the great markets of America and Europe; it has virtually no natural resources and must rely on imports; it is known for typhoons, earthquakes, deep snow, and other natural calamities; and it was defeated in World War II. There is nothing inevitable about Japan's economic success, but people's effort and ingenuity have surely contributed and quality control provided a sound methodology for improvement supported by those efforts and that ingenuity.

Is Everything Unique?

I have been engaged in quality control since its inception in Japan and have visited many companies. Even the list of names of all the different companies practicing QC is impressive. The electric and electronic industries have been practitioners of QC since the beginning. Precision instruments, metal, chemical, and raw material-related industries are also in the forefront in terms of QC.

When I first visit a company that has not yet adopted QC, I'm invariably told that it cannot do so because the industry is unique in some way. Any number of reasons are given to account for this uniqueness. Some companies claim they have too many different types of products to adopt QC. Others point out that they manufacture only a single item. Yet another group claims their products are governed by their raw materials, and that the quality of these raw materials is out of their control. But what company is *not* unique? Industries survive on the basis of their uniqueness. So whenever a company tells me it's unique, I pay no attention. As far as I'm concerned, there is no company or type of industry that cannot engage in quality control and benefit from it.

When quality control was first introduced in postwar Japan, it was believed that it was useful only in manufacturing, more specifically in factories, and that only a few types of industries were involved. Today far more types of industries engage in quality control than do not. The spread of QC has been quite typical. In any industry there is always one company that pioneers a new field. So once that company has begun to introduce quality control, it spreads to the rest of that industry like wildfire. This is just one more indication of the fierceness of competition in Japan. Basically, no matter which company or industry we consider, and no matter how "unique" it is, it can do what other Japanese companies and industries have done. To engage or not to engage in quality control — all that matters is the decision of top management.

Shafu — The Company's Way

Every company has its own way of doing things. In Japanese, we call this *shafu*. *Shafu* works in dramatic ways. As college students, company managers all spoke and acted alike. But five or six years later, they find themselves thinking, acting, and dressing very differently.

Immediately after graduation, I worked in a laboratory developing radar. One of the very first things I learned was that employees from different companies projected different images. Company A people looked and acted like technicians from the workplace; company B men were gentlemen and exceptionally polite; and at company C were the college professor types who always had to have the last word.

Each company's *shafu* is different, and whether a company has a good *shafu* or not can affect its performance. For this reason, some say that the first order of business for a new manager is to create a good *shafu*. It's that important. I will use my own experience to describe how *shafu* is created and nurtured.

Today Nippon Telegraph and Telephone (NTT) is a private company. When I first worked there, however, it was known as the Ministry of Communications. At that time it was no different from any other bureaucratic establishment. It was made a public corporation (*kosha*) in 1952 and became a private company in 1985. [Editor's note: In Japan a *kosha* or public corporation is run by the government.] Even before its privatization, it had become an unusual entity among the three public corporations and five government enterprises. Unlike the others, NTT was known for its entrepreneurial spirit and, clearly, a mere change of name from ministry to public corporation could not have brought this about. NTT had changed so much that it was said to employ more real businessmen than any other public corporation or government enterprise. This was due in large part to the superb administration of the late Dr. Tsuyoshi Kajii, NTT's first president.

When it became a public corporation, NTT was laboring under a huge deficit and had to become financially independent.

To that end, President Kajii began simplifying the organization as soon as he took over by eliminating unnecessary positions. Normally in Japanese organizations, the title of special consultant (*chosayaku*) is conferred on managers who would otherwise be let go when their services are no longer needed. Some government bureaus carried so many of these managers that people said that if you threw a stone, it would invariable land on some special consultant's head. At NTT, however, these extra managers were simply demoted. Division directors became section chiefs, and section chiefs became subsection chiefs. In this fashion 3,000 managers were demoted nationwide. The atmosphere at NTT became somewhat tense.

Next, President Kajii took measures to increase revenues. To provide incentives, he came up with a bookkeeping column, called the special account for income-increasing measures, which was credited in proportion to the increase in sales that it produced. It was a kind of rebate — the first ever given in a governmental agency since the founding of Japan as a nation! [Editor's note: This practice of creating a special account for the value of improvements is not limited to NTT. For example, between 1976 and 1985, Canon, Inc. accumulated over $500 million in what it terms "waste-elimination profit." These special "profits" are reinvested each year in new technology, equipment, and human resource development.]

The first group to register a surplus was a communications bureau in the western part of Japan. In those days, operators received requests for long distance calls and then placed them. Each time they received a request, the operators would ask if the caller wanted special handling. The fee for special handling was twice that of a normal call, but since everyone wanted their calls completed quickly, everyone asked for special handling anyway. So whenever a caller asked for special handling, the operators at this location went one step further and suggested "extra-special" handling.

No one from headquarters had told them to do this. Their only instruction had been to increase income, with the understanding that employees who responded would be recognized.

That incentive was all workers needed to begin thinking of ways to improve. When they saw the results, they worked even harder, and seemed to enjoy their work.

Mr. Kajii also changed the accounting method from a budget to an accounts-settlement system. Even today most government bureaus still rely on budgets. A bureau wins or loses depending on its budget. Once the budget is approved, one must simply use it well. In contrast, in the accounts-settlement system funds for projects are provided as needed, but results are scrutinized carefully later on. Under a budget-based system, people tend to feel that unless the budgeted amount is fully spent, something is lost. That is why, near the end of a fiscal year, managers may incur unnecessary expenses just to use up the budget.

Under an accounts-settlement system, however, this practice is eliminated. With the system in place at NTT, abuses such as the frequent "official travel" near the end of a fiscal year disappeared. Just by changing the accounting method in this fashion, NTT's *shafu* improved dramatically.

President Kajii's emphasis on increasing revenue as an incentive for employees is especially noteworthy because Japan's QC circles base their success on such incentives. In QC circles, creativity and inventiveness of the workers are acknowledged and "brought to life." Workers no longer feel like cogs in a machine; everyone feels that he or she is contributing something significant to the company.

Such enthusiasm and commitment are inspired and supported by company policy and objectives. That is why we say that a company's *shafu* is determined by its managers.

Management Objectives

NTT's experience illustrates how managers can change a company's *shafu* dramatically by establishing appropriate com-

pany objectives. But what are "objectives"? Objectives are standards we can set to evaluate whether a certain action is or is not
advisable for the company. Employees may not know how to act
in a given situation; objectives establish ground rules by which
to evaluate and choose among different courses of action.

Objectives must be simple, clear, correct, and honest if
everyone is to understand them. If objectives are couched in
the language of old-fashioned moral codes, they will have little
effect. If they require special interpretation, disputes about
meaning may arise. In that case, it is better not to have objectives at all. When a company's objective is simply to increase
revenues, however, everyone can understand it. With this
single objective, NTT regained its corporate strength within
two years.

New objectives do not have to be accompanied by detailed
instructions to rejuvenate an organization. Simplicity is the
key, and it is not confined to setting objectives. Even in an
otherwise well-managed company, the mere transfer of a section chief can suddenly change the atmosphere. The emergence
of a new leader often deeply affects the way people think — in
the workplace as well as the world.

When good objectives are set, the average worker will want
to follow them; however, if superiors establish objectives that
appear strange to the rest of the organization, they will be ig-
nored. This distinction is very important: To be effective, a top
manager must be able to issue timely, forward-looking objectives that respond to current conditions.

A company's way of doing things (shafu) is determined at the
top. If top management can establish basic objectives without
making any compromises, and if all the employees understand
these objectives, the company can move forward without further
intervention from the top. Furthermore, when these objectives
are also designed to promote creativity, nothing else is required.
Ultimately, the broad objectives established by top management become the moving force behind total quality control.

What Abilities Do Managers Need?

An organization can be transformed when a capable manager takes the helm. What are the abilities a good manager must have?

Specialized Knowledge: To begin with, a manager needs basic knowledge about the production process. This is expected of everyone, and the higher up the corporate ladder a manager is, the more knowledge he or she must have. That a manager majored in one of the liberal arts disciplines is no excuse for his or her inability to understand technical matters. Our life is long, and we spend only a few short years in college. To create such intellectual barriers is inappropriate behavior on the part of a manager. He or she must be willing to spend time learning about the industry.

General Knowledge: No matter how well-endowed with specialized knowledge, without general knowledge a manager may be thought of as "a fool in his own specialization."

Enthusiasm: No matter how rich in general and specialized knowledge, a person who lacks enthusiasm is ill-suited to become a manager. A manager may seem like a walking encyclopedia, but without a fighting spirit, he or she cannot lead subordinates.

Good Sense: Enthusiasm does not mean repeating the same thing over and over or scolding subordinates. A well-informed and motivated person who lacks good sense is probably the worst kind of manager. Who is a sensible manager? — A person with wisdom and good judgment.

Teamwork: Each manager is the head of his or her own organization. No matter how capable and enthusiastic, the manager who is not a team player cannot motivate his or her subordinates. Think about defense in the game of baseball: If the ball comes to second base the second baseman must catch it, but the shortstop also has an area of responsibility. If the ball is hit between infield and outfield, who should catch it? Teamwork means being ready to handle such contingencies. As soon as the ball is hit, the entire team must know who is responsible for catching it, and who will serve as backup. This understanding should not have to be explained, nor can it be disputed.

Fairness: Subordinates are always conscious of how their manager views them. If they have been treated unfairly, they are less willing to do their jobs. The higher up on the corporate ladder, the more a manager must be aware of the importance of fair-dealing with subordinates.

Understanding: This is the ability to grasp quickly and accurately what someone else is saying. A subordinate will soon lose interest if, after making a careful presentation, the manager's remarks are all irrelevant. Subordinates are willing to help out in difficult times as long as they feel that what they offer is understood and appreciated.

Power of Persuasion: No matter how good a plan is, if a manager is unable to persuade others to adopt it, it will go nowhere. Without the ability to speak persuasively it is impossible to manage others.

Stability: When a manager lacks self-confidence, subordinates may not know how to follow and act. A manager will lose subordinates unless he or she can carry out goals consistently, regardless of negative comments or criticism.

Courage: To implement a plan requires courage. Even when there are difficulties, however, subordinates will follow the example set by a courageous manager. Once goals are reached, employee morale will go up, and the manager will be seen as reliable by his or her own superiors. Management is always accompanied by certain risks; courage is an essential condition in facing those risks.

Good Health: A person who leads others must be healthy. A manager must be in good health to lead and provide a good example for others to follow.

Responsibility: Never blame subordinates for a failure; instead, assume responsibility for it yourself. And never take success away from a subordinate, give credit instead. According to opinion polls taken in Japan, workers prefer *naniwabushi*-oriented or "selfless" managers. That should come as no surprise! [Editor's note: *Naniwabushi* are folk tales in which leaders nobly bear the blame for others.]

Sensitivity: In any country, good human relations begin with sensitivity to the feelings of others. But never bring *personal* feelings into work — they may endanger the solidarity of the organization.

These are qualities a manager needs to administer an organization effectively, although perhaps only a super-person is endowed with all thirteen. Nonetheless we should think of these qualities as goals and not make too many excuses. The head of an organization is entrusted with the fate of each employee; that person has a grave responsibility and must strive to develop as many of these qualities as possible.

Finally, I have said that a company's *shafu* is created through objectives established by top management. A manager must always be thinking of appropriate objectives for subordinates and be able to demonstrate how they can be implemented.

The Role of Managers in Quality Control

No matter how many lectures on QC we attend, no matter how many books we read, we may end up knowing as little about QC as someone who knows nothing at all. Quality control is a discipline that can be mastered only through practice. The way to mastery is to go to the workplace and start working to eliminate one or two defects.

Some managers know all the catch phrases associated with QC and exhort their workers by talking at them; however, quality control is not *nembutsu*, that is, repeating prayers to obtain salvation. Quality control has its own special methodology, and if workers are expected to practice it, management must be able to show them how it's done.

In Japan, quality control has always meant the full participation of workers at the front line in the factory. We must not forget the other side of the coin, however, which is top management's active participation in QC. This is of the utmost importance. In company wide or total quality control (TQC), participation is not complete if only the workers but not managers are involved.

Moreover, "participation" must mean more than merely deciding to introduce quality control and bearing ultimate responsibility for it. Participation must be more than a formality. Top managers must certainly make the decision and provide the necessary support. Beyond that, however, top managers must be the first to *practice* quality control, to nurture a *shafu* that respects quality.

Internal audits or studies conducted to check the effectiveness of QC activities show that wherever QC has been successful, the essential ingredient has been active participation by top management. QC circle assemblies that report the results of QC activities within a company are commonplace, but their success or failure is also determined by the attitude of top management.

Top management commitment to quality control has been the key factor in its success in Japan. Without active enthusiasm from the top, QC simply cannot succeed on a company wide basis. If it is delegated to staff assistants, the movement invariably loses steam. Quality control conducted by assistants cannot guarantee the level of quality needed for company survival in today's fiercely competitive international environment.

CHAPTER 3

Productivity

Factors Creating an Abundant Society

In the late 1960s, when Japan entered a period of rapid economic growth, people in other countries began to call Japan an "economic animal." Many people felt that the Japanese used ugly, hard-sell methods to peddle their goods all over the world.

Why did Japanese products sell so well? The reason is actually very simple: They were quality products at a reasonable price. If they hadn't been so well-made and inexpensive, they would not have sold well, no matter how aggressively they were marketed. Japan's high growth economy has been sustained by its industrial power, which allows it to produce quality merchandise at low cost. What does industrial power mean?

Great Britain's automobile industry has yet to recover from the depressed state it fell into at the onset of the first energy crisis. Japanese-made cars, by contrast, are selling briskly, in some cases at amounts higher than the sticker price. The British government had considered imposing import restrictions on Japanese cars more than once. In the summer of 1975, however, an editorial in the *London Times* argued against import restrictions, on the basis that British cars were not selling simply because, unlike the Japanese, British automobile manufacturers were not offering the cars people wanted to buy.

(The same point could have been made about the American automobile industry in the early 1980s.)

This is real industrial power! We can talk about a worldwide depression or lack of resources, but industries with the power to produce useful merchandise prosper regardless of such conditions. This, in turn, increases the wealth of the society to which such industries belong.

Industrial Power

Some time ago, an employee of a Japanese trading company stationed in Africa gave me some interesting facts. New nations were becoming independent, and those new nations, almost without exception, wanted the most up-to-date factories. If a foreign advisor suggested building a factory more suitable to the current level of economic development, political leaders became angry, because they did not want to be looked down upon as members of a developing nation.

As might have been predicted, most of these up-to-date factories failed. A new factory must meet a host of conditions, and if it falls short even in one area, the whole system will fail. Without steady sales and supplies of raw materials, production will be erratic; furthermore, facilities become obsolete quickly and unless depreciated in an orderly fashion, the factory cannot continue to function; and if research and development cannot keep pace with the competition, sales will go downhill. These were the types of problems these "up-to-date" factories encountered.

When we speak of "industrial power" we immediately think of huge facilities and complicated machines. We must not forget, however, that before there can be facilities and equipment, we must have reliable ways to develop and sell steadily the merchandise produced by these machines. Capital must be available and workers trained carefully and managed efficiently. The many problems arising as a natural part of this process must be solved methodically. Finally, we must have the wisdom and fortitude needed to establish these conditions.

Consider the example of Switzerland — a fascinating country with a per capita income larger than that of the United States. Like Japan, however, Switzerland has very few natural resources. It does have snow and beautiful mountains good for attracting tourism. But snow and beautiful mountains could never create the highest per capita income in Europe.

Readers who visited the Swiss pavilion at Expo 70 in Osaka may recall the piston from the largest diesel engine in the world, an engine with 30,000 horsepower. It was placed just inside the entrance of the pavilion and stood as high as the ceiling. The piston was built by Sulzer Ltd., the top producer of the largest marine diesel engines in the world, in a country that has no access to the sea!

Switzerland is also known for its superiority in weapons manufacturing. During World War II, Japan's Zero fighter plane was famous for its superb capability. The cannon-like 20 mm machine guns on each wing could disintegrate a target fighter plane with one shot. These powerful long-range machine guns were built by Erikon of Switzerland.

We could cite numerous other examples to demonstrate the industrial power that has sustained Switzerland economically and given it the largest per capita income in Europe.

Highest Productivity in the World

Until recently, Europeans preferred to lease television sets since they broke down so often. It was difficult to get repairmen to make house calls, and sets often idled in the repair shop for as long as a month. Leasing a set meant prompt service; the leasing agents could not charge for a set that did not work, so they stood ready to make repairs or replace a set at the mere mention of an unclear picture. Once Japanese-made television sets were readily available, however, purchasing became a more attractive option. It was a natural development; even color TV sets made in Japan had a low rate of breakdown.

Here is another instructive story about Japanese-made televisions. In England, television service and repair is provided by a company that holds a maintenance contract with customers; in Japan, on the other hand, this service is provided by the vendor. Under the British system, service companies handle all makes of TV sets, so they have an idea of the breakdown rates by manufacturer. Naturally, these data were kept confidential.

In 1975, however, these breakdown rates were leaked to the press, causing quite a stir. Television sets made in Japan had been breaking down at a rate one-tenth to one-fifth that of American- and British-made sets. This publicity caused a large increase in sales of Japanese-made color sets in England. When the same information was published in American newspapers, Japanese TV sales went up in the U.S. as well. Japanese-made color TVs are simply the best in the world which is why they sell so well. No hard sell is necessary.

Until recently, many of the best-made products came from the United States. Now Japanese factories produce the highest-quality products of any country in the world, and not just in the field of home entertainment. Japanese tourists no longer bring wristwatches home from overseas, nor do they prefer foreign-made cameras. The high quality of Japanese-made steel is also well known. Japanese-made motorbikes and pianos, too, rank at the top. In shipbuilding, Japan's supremacy is longstanding. There are countless other examples. And, in 1980, Japan also became the world's largest producer of automobiles.

Will Inflation Continue?

Here is something important to consider. The continuing threat of inflation creates social problems in many countries. In the late 1970s, for example, there was a period of "stagflation," a time of stagnation combined with inflation when prices continued to rise even when business conditions were poor. Many Japanese gave up on Japan's economy in 1974 during the first oil crisis. People became pessimistic because the future appeared bleak, and newspapers began to talk about "uncontrollable price increases." With the price of crude oil suddenly jumping 400 percent and Japan's industry depending almost exclusively on energy from oil, such pessimism was understandable. Living standards, it seemed, could never improve under such conditions, no matter how large a wage increase one received. In the annual spring wage negotiations, the cost of living increase became a key factor. The actual increase in prices was mixed, however. Table 3 compares the prices of various goods in June 1970 and April 1986. The data are taken from newspapers, retail price indexes and industry, among other sources.

Inside Inflation

The mass media would have us believe that everything is becoming more and more expensive, but the table reveals that prices have not gone up consistently with inflation; some consumer goods prices even fell in the 16-year period.

For example, automobile prices rose by 60 to 70 percent. Since the newer models are equipped with anti-pollution devices to meet the most stringent requirements in the world and other options have been added, the *actual* price increase may have been as little as 10 percent. And the price of TV sets and refrigerators is at the same level as 16 years ago.

You might think, with these examples in mind, that only highly processed goods remained stable or dropped in price between 1970 and 1986. In the raw material industries, prices for steel plate, synthetic fiber, and cement, for example, doubled. However, taking into account the 1,000 percent increase in the price of crude oil, these figures seem quite reasonable.

There was a time when the price of eggs accurately reflected the overall inflationary trend, but foodstuffs, led by eggs and including pork, did not double. Cheese, which is a milk product, merely rose at the same rate as eggs, far below what might be expected. The price of pork, eggs, and chicken in Japan has remained consistent with prices worldwide. There was a sharp

	1970	1986	% (86/70)
Passenger Car (1300/cc engine)	521,000	883,000	169
Black and white TV	44,000 (12")	50,000 (14")	113
Refrigerator	94,000 (185 l)	110,000 (170 l)	117
Single-lens reflex camera (F2)	48,000	83,000	173
Color film (36 exp.)	580	780	134
1.6 mm steel plate (ton)	43,000	83,000	983
Rayon yarn (453 g)	155	*	
Cement (ton)	7,960	12,700	160
Rice (producer price; 60 kg)	8,994	17,557	195
Whisky (aged)	1,900	3,170	167
Cheese (0.5 lb.)	168	310	185
Eggs (1 kg wholesale)	194	360	186
Pork (medium grade,1 kg wholesale)	890	1,500	169
Broiler chicken	757	1,130	149
Beef (1 kg wholesale)	1,350	3,510	260
Horse mackerel (kg)	357	1,580	443
Suit (retail price)	22,000	69,000	314
Condominium (three-bedrooms)	8,000,000	**	
Haircut	543	2,688	495
Home electricity (1 kw)	10.17	23.55	232
Telephone (1 unit)	7	10	143
National (1 km) railway ticket	4.2	16.2	386
Newspaper subscription (1 month)	750	2,800	373
Weekly magazine	70	220	314
National theater	2,000	5,000	250
Average monthly pay	64,000	280,000	438

* In 1986, this item was no longer readily available in retail outlets.
** With the sharp rise in the price of land, regional differences in pricing further widened, making it impossible to provide a figure meaningful enough for comparison.

**Table 3. Price Change (in Yen) in Consumer Products: 1970-1986
(1986 Price as Percent of 1970 Price)**

increase in the price of mackerel and beef. In general, however, no clear pattern emerges in the behavior of consumer prices in this period.

By contrast, prices in the service sector rose significantly. In 1986, it cost close to five times as much to get a haircut as in 1970. Similarly, the price of a one-month subscription to a newspaper rose by 370 percent.

For many of us in Japan, housing is the most important issue today. The price of condominiums more than tripled between 1970 and 1980 and continued to rise sharply thereafter. Also, fares for railroad travel rose nearly 400 percent. Generally speaking, highly processed industrial products have risen in price far less than labor-intensive services, which have risen very sharply.

Reduce Prices by Increasing Productivity

In the 16-year period under discussion, wages in Japan, like the cost of services, more than quadrupled. That does not mean that wages fell for workers involved in the production of goods that dropped or remained relatively low in price. Their wages rose as much as everyone else's — in some instances even more.

How can a company raise the salaries and wages of its workers without raising the price of its product? Very simply, by increasing productivity. On the average, Japanese productivity increased 325 percent in the period under consideration; and in some industrial sectors, the increase was over 400 percent. If productivity increases by 400 percent or more, salaries and wages can be raised by that much and the price of goods can still be lowered. For example, the price of a car tripled, at most, while salaries more than quadrupled between 1970 and 1980. That is how, in Japan, a new employee, fresh out of college, can afford a new car.

The average base pay of ordinary Japanese workers ranks high compared with average wages in the United States and European countries. If we add benefits, Japanese wage levels may actually be ahead of those of the United States.

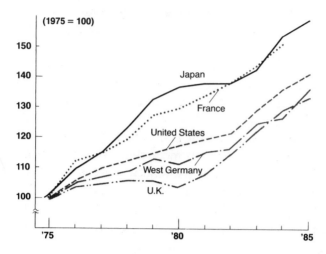

Source: Bank of Japan, *Comparative International Statistics* (1986)

Figure 1. Trends in Labor Productivity in Manufacturing Sector (1975-1985)

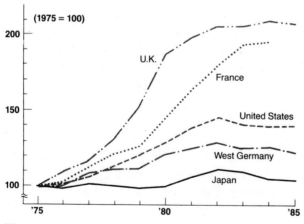

Wage cost index = wage index ÷ labor productivity index
Source: Bank of Japan, *Comparative International Statistics* (1986)

Figure 2. Trends in Wage Cost Index in Manufacturing Sector (1975-1985)

Japanese cities are now flooded with cars. Japanese tourists visiting foreign countries bump into other Japanese tourists, demonstrating Japan's prosperity, which was made possible by the increase in productivity.

Are Today's Young People Really Not Up to Par?

In Japan the older generation often says that people *used* to work hard but that nowadays many younger people do not. In the "old days" people certainly worked very hard — because of their lower level of productivity. Had they not worked so hard, they could not have survived. It doesn't necessarily follow that today's young people are lazy or not hard working.

High productivity is a characteristic of modern society. Today's workers have to work only five days a week; they drive their own cars and can spend their leisure time at home watching TV in air-conditioned comfort — all because the productivity of Japanese society has risen tremendously.

The Economic Planning Agency of Japan recently completed a survey of the benefits of the five-day work week compared to the five-and-a-half-day work week practiced by many Japanese companies. According to the survey, prices have increased at a proportionately lower rate in industries practicing a five-day work week for more than a decade. This survey certainly does not suggest that the "lazier" an industry, the lower its rate of price increase; it does say, however, that when productivity goes up, work hours can be shortened and wages raised without raising the price of the products.

If America finds itself trapped in an inflationary spiral, the only solution is to increase productivity. Americans seem to have trouble implementing this solution, even though national consensus now exists that higher productivity is the only remedy for inflation.

Yet the Japanese people somehow have not internalized this basic principle either — even though our own example pro-

	Year	Japan	United States	West Germany	France	Great Britain	Italy
Crude Steel	1985	14.7	11.2	5.7	2.6	2.2	3.3
Cement	1984	8.8	7.9	3.2	2.6	**	4.3
Plastics	1976*	17.7	35.8	11.6	7.4	5.8	6.5
Synthetic Fibre	1985	11.3	20.1	5.7	1.3	2.1	3.8
Automobiles	1985	27.2	25.8	9.9	6.7	2.9	3.5
Television	1976*	29.9	13.7	6.5	3.1	3.7	3.2
Ships	1986	43.6	**	2.4	**	**	2.7

Source: Kokuseisha, Statistical Data for Japan, 1987, and Economic White Paper, 1980.
 * Older data are given to show the relative strengths of these countries before the onset of competition from the newly industrialized nations.
** Data for the given year not available.

Table 4. Japan's Share of World Production

vided the evidence on which it is based! Some may feel that appealing to it is old-fashioned. But when you think about it, we never appreciated the importance of water or air either until we learned about pollution. In the same way, even Japan, which has experienced wave after wave of increases in productivity in the postwar period, today has a compelling need to re-examine the importance of productivity.

CHAPTER 4

How to Raise Productivity

The Three Ways

I'd like to begin by clearing up a misunderstanding. In Japan, many people still believe that raising productivity requires workers to work longer hours. This view comes from not understanding what productivity means. When we increase the number of hours of work and thus produce more goods, we are increasing *production*, not productivity.

Productivity is the result of efficiency. If an item that takes ten hours to produce can be produced in five hours under a new system, productivity has doubled. Increasing productivity actually means the opposite of longer work hours: Make a job easier and complete it sooner — only then does productivity rise. There must be no confusion about this.

Now the question is one of method. Is it possible to make jobs enjoyable and also increase the speed with which they are done? Some people may doubt this is possible, but there are ways.

Looking back in history, we see that productivity has risen steadily. Indeed, I'd venture to say that everything that has contributed to the modernization of industry has actually been a means of raising productivity. Analyze these various methods and you will find that they fall into three basic categories: *mechanization*, *specialization*, and *management techniques*.

Mechanization

The first step towards productivity improvement involves mechanization.

If we intend to transport a product that weighs 50 kilograms, we must remember that no one can carry such a weight very far. If we put the same object on a bicycle cart, even a child can move it. This means that productivity has been increased.

Specialization

Mechanization

The super-express Tokaido bullet train between Tokyo and Osaka went into operation in October 1964. Before then, even an express train took seven hours or more to cover the distance, so business people were forced either to stay overnight at their destination or to sleep on the train. Once the new bullet train went into service, they could travel between the two cities and return home the same day. Consequently, a person could accomplish twice as much work. In other words, productivity improved substantially, thanks to mechanization.

Today, in films from developing countries, we see men carrying heavy loads on their shoulders, and the sweat on their brows is clearly visible. It goes against the principle of respect for humanity to ask someone to carry heavy loads, and it is a sorry state of affairs when work that can be done by machines is still done manually.

Japan is the world leader in automation. About 70 percent of all robots are located there. It has the highest degree of mechanization in both television manufacturing and shipbuilding.

The table below contains figures from various countries with regard to their robotization. They were taken from statistics compiled by the Robot Institute of America. It is clear from this table that Japan's high productivity comes from its exceptionally high rate of mechanization. After all, mechanization remains one of the most important factors in productivity and economic development.

Specialization

People are born with different talents. If we can select the people most suited for a job, train them and give them the chance to do good work, productivity will improve significantly. "The right person for the right job" is a meaningful phrase. When employees are allowed to specialize, work goes more smoothly and productivity can increase many times over. If we give a job to the wrong person, however, nothing is accomplished, and productivity equals zero. This is what is meant by the term *specialization*.

Machines are not flexible. Once they are installed, they cannot do more than they were designed to do, no matter how new

	1980	1982	1983	1984
Japan	14,250	31,900	41,265	67,300
U.S.A.	4,100	6,300	9,400	14,500
Germany, F.R.	1,420	4,300	4,800	6,600
France	600	993	2,010	3,380
Italy	353	1,100	2,000	2,700
U.K.	371	977	1,753	2,623
Sweden	940	1,450	1,900	2,400
Czechoslovakia	—	154	1,845	—
Canada	250	273	700	
Australia	—	—	528	—
Norway	170	—	—	—

Table 5. Total Population of Robots

and sophisticated they may be. People, on the other hand, can perform widely differing tasks depending on the job they are given. If employees are well suited for their jobs and happy in them, they may increase productivity ten or even 100 times.

Many overseas observers attribute the high productivity of Japanese workers to their high level of education and intelligence. The Japanese are supposed to be smarter than everyone else and thus more productive. But the Japanese are no smarter than people elsewhere, nor do they have greater manual dexterity. The real answer lies in the high morale of Japanese workers. They are well educated, but they are also willing to work.

Management Techniques

Mechanization deals with things, while specialization deals with human resources. Combining people and things effectively involves *management*. We may have similar facilities and people but, depending on how we manage these two factors, our results can be quite different.

Suppose cars had to stop at every corner for red lights. If the lights were synchronized to turn green with the speed of the traffic, travel time could be cut in half. Translated into production terms, this means that productivity is doubled.

The cars, the highway, and the people in the cars are the same, only one fact is different: traffic lights are synchronized with traffic flow. Adding this sort of improvement is a function of management.

To eliminate congestion on a highway, we can either build another one or widen the existing one with additional lanes. These techniques are similar to the method of facility investment. Building another highway in an urban area involves enormous costs; instead, we could install a computer-controlled traffic signal system, at a minimal cost by comparison.

Two companies may produce the same types of goods, with essentially identical facilities and equipment and about the same number of workers. Depending on the company, however, their finished products may be quite different with regard to quality, cost, and productivity.

Suppose one company makes no additional investment in equipment or changes in the labor force. Yet by introducing some new way of doing things, quality, cost, and productivity begin to exceed those of the other company. Again, management techniques are responsible for the difference.

QC as a Management Technique

When the consumer movement was at its height, some groups demanded that manufacturers make public the cost of their products. They had seen the finished products and believed the costs for similar products to be the same. But even identical products from one factory will differ in cost depending on the quantity of the run produced and the combination of processes. This is common knowledge to anyone who has ever worked in manufacturing. The consumer groups would not have made these demands had they had some knowledge of what management in manufacturing involves.

In the Toyota production system, the required parts must be delivered at the time and in the quantity needed, "just-in-time." If this is done properly, manufacturing can proceed without inventory. Costs are lowered, and considerable savings are realized. If the system functions well, defects will also be reduced. Clearly a system like this is based on principles inherent in management.

There are other approaches to management, such as industrial engineering (IE), value engineering (VE), and operations research (OR). Each method was introduced as a way of modernizing industry and has been implemented successfully. If we examine them for a common denominator we find that, no matter what their distinct goals, they seek improvement through *data*. Thus, a person who has mastered quality control should have no trouble applying any of the other methods. In any case, an industry need not be concerned about what its improvement activity is called. It can be QC, OR, or IE. What *is* important is that productivity is improved.

Quality control, however, has developed special tools. To obtain good results, we cannot engage in quality control and rely on methods of our own choosing. Anyone who has ever played the game of chess or Go (*shogi*) knows it is possible to reach the first level of understanding alone, but that's about it. To gain real skill in these games, we must study and master the basic steps (*joseki*). Similarly, in quality control there are special basic steps. When these steps are mastered, improvement comes naturally.

Quality Control Does *Not* Mean High Cost

Some people mistakenly believe that quality control means greater cost. They reason that although quality control makes it possible to manufacture better products they will be more expensive because high-quality products usually are. Simply put, the argument goes: No matter how efficiently high-quality products are produced, we must lose out in the cost competition. So whether or not we engage in quality control, we don't acquire any advantage.

To resolve this misunderstanding, we need note only that those Japanese industries that are competitive in quality around the world are also competitive in terms of cost. What must be underscored is that if QC is introduced successfully and reduces defects, costs will not increase but decrease — and by a very substantial amount.

Some people may say this is too good to be true, but I can cite many real-life examples to support my claim. I will go so far as to say that any company that insists it must charge more for its products because it is practicing quality control should be regarded with suspicion. That company probably isn't engaged in quality control at all.

By the same token, it is wrong to assume that quality control does not cost anything. There are always some costs when mechanization or employee training is involved. In the case of quality control, they will be related to introducing it and ensuring that it succeeds. But like mechanization and specialization, quality control produces savings many times larger than these expenses. QC must be implemented thoroughly, however. If you are only half committed to it, you cannot get the results you want and if you abandon it half-way through, you will be throwing away good money and getting nothing for your investment.

Let's look at an actual example of how costs were cut with the introduction of quality control.

Cutting Costs in Half

An electric parts manufacturer produces a special kind of electrolytic condenser by etching an oxidized membrane on aluminum foil to create something similar to alumite and then rolling the membrane into the shape of a condenser. Once this is done the work is complete. Most of the cost is in materials (initially 68 percent) so, generally, no matter how much the process is rationalized, the cost cannot fall below that level.

This type of condenser also happens to be difficult to produce. At the time I was asked to help organize a quality control program at this company, production was 200,000 per month. We pursued the program with vigor, and only four months later, defective units were down to one-tenth the previous quantity and the basic cost was cut in half. You might ask how this was possible since 68 percent of the original cost was materials. The answer is simple:

Monthly production was 200,000 units. To produce this much output, however, it was necessary to manufacture 280,000 units because the defect rate was 30 percent, all of which was consigned to scrap. By eliminating 90 percent of the defective units, production and materials costs of nearly 72,000 units were avoided.

In the midst of the program, demand began to pick up. We increased monthly production to 550,000 units, without expanding facilities or adding personnel. How did we do this?

When the defect rate was 30 percent, our machines had to be stopped repeatedly to change materials or adjust the level of fluids. Workers had to remain near the machines and "nurse" them. Once the defect rate was down to one-tenth, however, the machines could be run almost without interruption. Now, with the same capacity, but running uninterruptedly, the machines could produce 550,000 units per month. Costs were cut in half.

There are two factors that tend to reduce costs under QC.

1. Output that otherwise goes to waste is marketable.

2. Production can be increased using the same equipment.

Think of what happens when you drive your car on a poorly maintained road — obviously, you must reduce speed while, on a well-paved highway, you can progress faster. That's what it's like — but you have to experience the improvement to really understand it. Quality control can work wonders for an organization and the many successful Japanese products bear witness to this fact.

CHAPTER 5

Statistical Quality Control

Two Qualities, Two Technologies

What does the word "quality" mean? It is commonly used in two senses.

It refers to the capability designed into a product. Sports cars and passenger cars, for example, have distinctive differences; they are designed to be different. Unlike passenger cars, sports cars can reach very high speeds on an expressway. Of course, sports cars are higher priced and more expensive to maintain. "Quality" used in this context indicates the features that make sports cars desirable over ordinary passenger cars. These desirable features are built in by design, however. To compare two items designed for different purposes in terms of "quality" is like comparing apples and oranges.

If, on the other hand, a product lacks some of the "qualities" originally specified for it, we say it is of poor quality; it was not produced as it should have been. "Quality" in this sense can be thought of as *serviceability*, *fitness*, or *reliability*. This sort of quality determines whether a product can be used with confidence.

No matter how beautiful a sports car may be, if its engine stops in the middle of a race, it is not serviceable. If the car squeaks continually or if it spends more time in the shop than on the road, the car is of poor quality, no matter what its rating.

A reliable or "high quality" car, on the other hand, will run as long as it has fuel in its tank, regardless of how roughly it is treated. The primary task in quality control is to enhance this second type of "quality."

Lately, people have been saying that it is self-serving and arrogant of the Japanese to imagine that their technology is at the forefront just because Japan's automobile industry is so advanced. For example, we have only to look at America's space program, they say, to realize how far behind Japan is in advanced technologies.

But such arguments miss the point. There is more than one kind of technology. Technology that creates the function of a product and technology that creates its quality are two different things. In the techniques that produce Olympic athletes, Japan is behind the United States in many areas. But in QC, Japan has succeeded where others have not. Whatever level of technology Japan achieves, it can claim to be second to none in terms of quality and cost. This by itself is a kind of technology, something we call *management*.

Why Produce Defects?

What are the general principles for improving serviceability? Before we can answer that question, we must understand how defects are produced.

Whenever many defective items are produced in a factory, we ask the following questions: Are the raw materials appropriate? Are the machines functioning correctly? Have the workers made any mistakes? Eventually, we find the cause or causes of defects and hopefully eliminate them.

Dr. Walter A. Shewhart, who created what we know today as statistical quality control, looked at these problems another way. Shewhart saw the cause of defects in the wide variation in the quality of units actually manufactured. What would happen to the defect rate if we could eliminate this variability or inconsistency in output, so that whether ten or 100 units were produced they would be identical? The rate would be either zero or 100 percent — all items would be either good or defective. In the manufacturing process, however, the rate always falls somewhere between zero and 100 percent. In other words, there is always some inconsistency — no two units are ever identical.

This phenomenon is easier to understand with the help of a bar graph. In Figure 3, the horizontal or x-axis represents the desired quality characteristic, e.g., size, weight, purity, and so on, expressed as a numerical value.

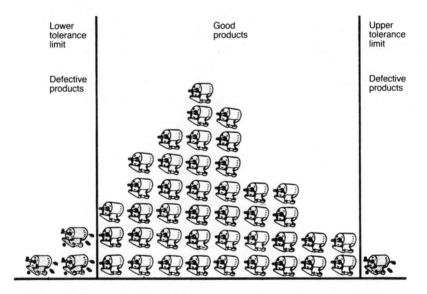

Figure 3.

If some point on the x-axis is designated the target value for production, most of the output will be within a certain range on either side of the target. Some units may be above it, some below; the farther from the target, the fewer the number of units.

The resulting diagram is called a histogram. We limit the range of acceptable units around the target by setting endpoints — the upper and lower tolerance limits. Units that end up outside these limits (shaded in the diagram) are the defective ones.

Note that in drawing the histogram, there is no need to be concerned with its shape. It may look as pretty as a mountain, as ours does, it may be compressed, or it may have two summits.

Eliminating Defects through Inspection

Now how do we eliminate the defective units? Selective inspection is one method, in which units that do not meet specifications are excluded. When the inspection is complete, the histogram assumes the shape shown in Figure 4-A. All the remaining units are within specifications and thus considered good products.

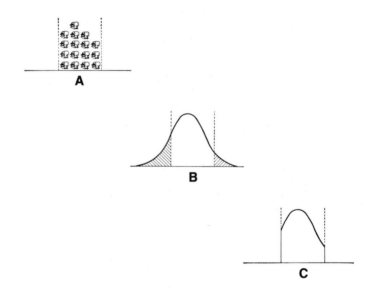

Figure 4.

The point is easier to comprehend if we use a line graph in place of the bar graph in our histogram.

Figure 4-B shows the condition before inspection and Figure 4-C, the condition afterwards. Inspection is a bit like plastic surgery; it simply cuts off what is not wanted.

Costs invariably increase, however, when quality is assured in this manner. Some units must be scrapped, others must be reworked.

If there is variation in manufactured products, it is natural to assume that there must also be variation in inspection methods. No matter how hard they try, inspectors cannot be certain that they have eliminated every single defective unit. Moreover, they may inadvertently reject perfectly good units.

If we reject good units during inspection, quality assurance becomes even more expensive, so selective inspection is not a very good method. When dispersion is high, however, it is the only way to assure quality. In fact, when this method is employed, a company may declare some units "special exceptions" when there are shortages or delays in meeting delivery dates. "Special exceptions" is a euphemism for defective units that have been labelled accepted — it is a risky practice, especially if specifications are reasonable. The manufacturer may later regret the decision to market so-called "special exceptions" when complaints start to come in and losses of several times the original cost of a unit mount up.

Another Method

Inspection is a classical means of quality assurance (QA). Dr. Shewhart, however, promoted another very simple method of eliminating defectives. Imagine shooting arrows at a target. A beginner will frequently hit wide of the mark; that is, there will always be some dispersion, naturally. If this dispersion can be eliminated, through practice and proper technique, for example, then every arrow will hit the bull's-eye.

In this method we eliminate defects by changing the *shape* of the dispersion rather than by performing "surgery" on the dispersion curve. Dr. Shewhart named this method *statistical quality control*. He used the word "statistical" since statistics is the discipline that deals with dispersion.

The American movie *Annie Get Your Gun* was a big hit in Japan. Annie Oakley typifies this simple principle of Japanese quality control: a "good shot" does not waste a single round, and this brings the cost down. But how do we become "good shots"? What can we do to change the shape of a dispersion? We know what must be accomplished, but without a concrete tool, this knowledge is useless.

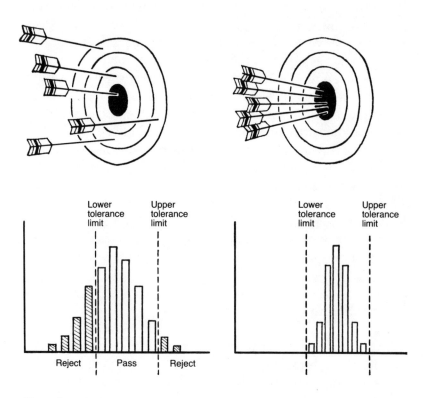

Figure 5.

Degree of Contribution

We tend to assume that products we produce with the same materials, processing, and assembly methods will be identical. Materials are not uniform in quality, however, and with different qualities of materials the results are bound to vary. Also, we will get different products if processing conditions or assembly methods vary even a little. With dispersion in each aspect of production overlapping, the final dispersion becomes even greater.

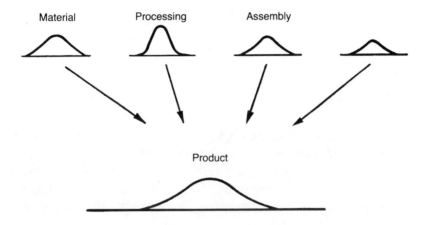

Figure 6.

To eliminate the final dispersion, we must eliminate all the inconsistencies that have contributed to it. Only then will dispersion in output disappear. To eliminate every source of dispersion is a difficult task, however, and it invariably increases costs. Of course, if we don't care whether we increase costs, we may as well not do quality control — conventional inspection is much faster. Unless quality improves and costs decline, it makes no sense to engage in quality control.

A key concept in narrowing the final dispersion introduced by Shewhart is the idea of *contribution rate*.

Inconsistency in products, Shewhart tells us, results from various factors in production. The way in which these factors affect the product and the degree to which they affect it are different in each case. For example, in plating, the temperature of a solution can go up or down without any visible impact on the plate; however, if the current density changes even slightly, the color of the finish will be uneven.

Shewhart called these differing rates of influence the "degree of contribution." He advocated stabilizing the factors that contributed to the largest degree first, even if more time or money was involved in resolving the various problems. In this way, the quality of finished products would also be stabilized.

Statistically Controlled State

At this point someone is bound to present me with data like that in Figure 7 and propose the following: "Dispersion disappeared when we eliminated the causes of inconsistency as you suggested, but now all the finished units are bunched together outside the lower tolerance limit (L), which means that we have a 100 percent defect rate. Before, the output looked like M but had excessive dispersion; but thanks to this dispersion, at least some of our output was acceptable."

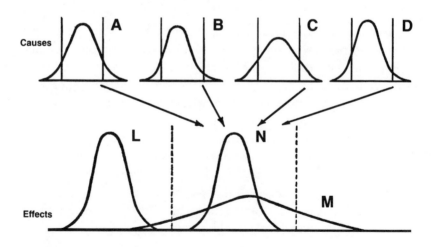

Figure 7.

If the entire output falls into category L, the defect rate is indeed 100 percent. But there is nothing to worry about in that case. When conditions change so there is less dispersion (from

M to L), the people practicing QC have discovered the real reason for the dispersion, the case of the major degree of contribution. If this were not so, the dispersion could not have been reduced. In other words, if the degree of contribution of a cause is significant, when conditions responsible for this cause change, the change in results is also significant. In our example, factor A is identified as the major cause of dispersion. By changing A, the quality of the finished unit changes. Now if we want the quality of the unit to fall within the tolerance limits, we have only to shift A — we can change the results by changing the factors.

By locating the major causes of dispersion, product quality can be shifted from right to left or from left to right; we can even widen or narrow the amount of dispersion. Once we reach this state, the quality is said to be controlled, that is, quality control has been attained.

Dr. Shewhart called this the *controlled state*. In statistical quality control we eliminate defects by identifying and controlling the factors that affect quality. In other words, unless we catch all the culprits causing dispersion, it is impossible to control quality. To do anything else runs counter to the basic principles of quality control.

Shewhart's Statistical Quality Control

To summarize Shewhart's approach to quality control:

1. *Catch the culprits of dispersion (process analysis).* Identify the factors of dispersion. When many factors are involved, study the impact each one has on dispersion; this is called its degree of contribution. To assess the impact of each cause, use data collected at the workplace, never rely on theory.

2. *Place the culprit in custody (standardization).* Once we have isolated a major cause, we place it under surveillance and control, that is, we try to stabilize it as much as possible.

3. *Watch the culprit to prevent escape (process control).* In process control, we prevent the recurrence of major causes by making sure the factors causing dispersion stay within the proper limits.

In principle, if we cannot control the causes of dispersion, we have no quality control. In such a factory, defects can appear at any point in the production cycle. If daily data on production were graphed, defect rates would be unstable, up one day and down the next like a kite without a tail. In QC, reducing and eventually eliminating defects is essential; however, this cannot be achieved simply by telling the workers to do so.

We endeavor to stabilize quality by identifying the causes of dispersion and then reducing defects. Success comes when dispersion has become so small as to be insignificant.

Put simply, QC is a little like hiring an expert marksman for the company. If not even one arrow misses the target, costs invariably come down. When another target appears, our expert marksman can shoot it down at once. Once all processes are in the controlled state, the company is able to manufacture any product it wants. Bear in mind that truly high-quality products do not vary in quality; customers can purchase them with confidence.

A company striving to produce serviceable, reliable products is also in the process of optimizing quality in product capability. This is why Japanese-made cars, watches, televisions, and cameras are regarded as high-quality products throughout the world.

Without QC, there can be no high-quality products.

CHAPTER 6

Problem Solving

Let the Data Speak

Our basic approach in quality control is to locate the "culprits," or causes of dispersion by gathering data. Some causes may *sound* reasonable in theory but should never be accepted as real without data. By the same token, once the data have been studied, we may realize that totally unsuspected causes have a significant degree of contribution.

When we begin to practice quality control, we often find true causes in the most improbable factors. This actually makes a lot of sense. If major cause factors were easy to locate, they would have been discovered and neutralized long ago. In fact, no one ever knows what these causes are, which is why no serious steps are taken to eliminate them.

Sometimes it helps not to have too much specialized product and process knowledge. If we look just at the data, causes of dispersion may be quite obvious; but experts, blinded by their own expertise, may be unable to discern them. When studying data it helps to be open-minded, unhampered by special knowledge or over-familiarity with the conditions in the workplace. Often, people who have never worked in the factory that is having the problems make the best detectives.

The data must be "true," that is, we must never let it "lie." If the atmosphere in the workplace prevents the real data from being exposed, the causes of dispersion will never be uncovered. Quality control is premised on the assumption that all data are interpreted honestly.

This also means that data must be used only to catch the causes of dispersion. Otherwise, we may get into the habit of saying only what will please superiors and colleagues. In such an atmosphere, true data may never emerge. Some workers may even refuse to cooperate in gathering data.

Everyone in QC knows how dangerous false information can be. Taking improvement measures on the basis of false information can result in costly mistakes. A doctor cannot make an accurate diagnosis if the patient is lying. Certainly, a sick person would rather be cured than die, but sometimes the nature of the illness may be too embarrassing to reveal. Treatment takes longer when true causes are not revealed. We should think of defects as a kind of illness and promote an attitude within the organization that will help us collect accurate data.

A Tale about Tuners

The tuner is usually the first element of a television set to malfunction. Electronic push-button sets are now common, but in the past all channel selectors had to be turned by hand and could malfunction if the tuner had a poor contact.

The tuner is the point where electric waves are first picked up. Standardized tuners were mass-produced and used in many different types of television sets. Some time ago, a quality control expert investigated the malfunction rate of tuners. He found that although identical tuners were used, the malfunction rate differed considerably from model to model. He realized that the problem had to be related to something other than the tuner; however, he still had the problem of discovering the true factor among many possible alternatives. People use their television sets in different ways; some place them in dusty corners, others keep them in their living room, more or less as an ornament. Frequency of use and the source of electricity can also differ. Thus, a TV breakdown could be caused by the environment or a simple error in the manufacturing process. Data collected from thousands and thousands of sets revealed, however, that tuners broke down according to the type of television set in which they had been installed.

The quality control expert looked at the data from many different angles and factored in every conceivable condition and its relation to the breakdown rate: was it related to cabinet size, for example, or to a temperature increase, the length of the tuner shaft or the difference in units of electric current? For a long time there seemed to be no correlation between any of the factors, but finally the cause emerged.

The correlation lay in the distance from the tuner to the speaker. The closer the tuner was to the speaker, the more often it broke down; the farther away, the lower the malfunction rate. Once this correlation had been established, manufacturers started to place speakers as far away from the tuners as possible in the cabinet, with the result that customer complaints were reduced dramatically.

It is still not clear from a technical perspective why locating the tuner close to the speaker causes it to malfunction. We do know that they should be kept as far apart as possible, and that is all we need to know to achieve success.

Two Approaches

In general, there are two ways to discover the causes of defects. The first is to employ theoretical principles discovered and studied by *sempai* (teachers — engineers who studied the field before us) to search for cause-and-effect relationships. Since this approach utilizes established investigative techniques, it is called the method of technical analysis by some people. It is an effective method that has brought about many good results. There are situations, however, when this method cannot help us.

The second method, based on statistical analysis, allows us to find effective measures without understanding any theoretical

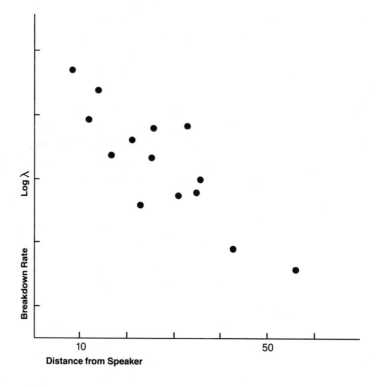

Figure 8.

cause-and-effect relationships. A problem like the malfunctioning tuner, for example, cannot be solved in a laboratory no matter how much data is accumulated; nor can it be anticipated by an engineer creating scenarios for failure at a desk. The relationship between one factor and the malfunction became clear only after we had collected data from tens of thousands of TV sets in actual use.

The approach is to collect as much data as possible on the possible causes. The data may be full of discrepancies, but if properly organized and averaged, they will cancel each other out, and significant differences will emerge. This is an example of the application of the law of large numbers. In terms of clarity of application, it is almost a textbook case.

In keeping with the first approach, many people believe that causes must be discovered before defects can be corrected and eliminated. As the tuner case illustrates, however, we do not always need to know causes in order to reduce defects. When we conduct campaigns to eliminate defects in the workplace, we often discover countermeasures before we understand the cause.

When we look for the causes of defects using statistical quality control, we typically gather the data and let it tell us what we need to know. This is called control based on the facts, or *fact control*. We could begin with an idea instead — many scientific theories can be brought forward to account for a problem in manufacturing. Unless a theory actually reduces defects when put into practice, however, it is of no use.

Problem Solving

Statistics can help us find ways to reduce defects even if we are unable to investigate the mechanisms that cause them in the first place.

Some time ago, I presented a year-long televised seminar on the Japan Broadcasting Corporation (NHK) network. We celebrated the end of the year with a party at the station. I still remember a remarkable statement the producer of the show made on that occasion. He declared that everything I had said over the year was simple and consistent with common sense. Only one thing had really impressed him: the sequence in which problems are solved through QC, starting from the point at which a problem is selected to when it is solved. "Isn't this sequence the very essence of quality control?" he asked.

I thought about the question and realized that he had penetrated to the heart of the matter. Quality control is a *methodology* for conducting improvement activities. Most academic disciplines simply impart new knowledge; in quality control, however, the knowledge imparted provides us with tools for improvement. Even more importantly, we use these tools to train people in problem solving.

Quality control is a challenging and unique occupation. I have been asked to help metalworks producing zinc, copper, steel, and tungsten. I have also been asked to help manufacturers of watches, cameras, electric appliances, paper, and rubber. Conventional wisdom would call for a specialist on metallurgy to be a consultant for a zinc factory and a mechanical engineer for a watchmaker. But a quality control consultant goes anywhere, making difficulties disappear as if by magic!

It is helpful for a QC specialist to have some knowledge about the mechanics or principles of production in the client industry. But this knowledge provides only background information and hints about what to investigate. Sometimes, a QC specialist is more effective when he or she knows nothing about the factory in question. With no preconceptions, the specialist can investigate every aspect of the factory without prejudice. A little knowledge, on the other hand, can be dangerous. The specialist may become preoccupied with it and overlook something fundamental. When we gather data without knowing the fundamentals, we will never get any answers no matter how hard we try. This is like criminal investigation — the detective who studies only useless leads never solves the crime.

The Sequence in Problem Solving

The statistical method is like a magic wand for one simple reason. The discipline of statistics teaches us how to identify a problem and the sequence in which it is to be solved. Some people may still feel that statistics is little more than sleight of hand. Let me show what the tricks really are.

In practicing quality control, having data is far more important than knowing the principles of the manufacturing process. The QC specialist who visits the factory and gets data that helps distinguish between good and defective products has accomplished the first step in problem solving. In this step, he or she has noted all the conditions involved in manufacturing both good and defective products — for example, materials, manufacturing conditions, differences in machines, employee work habits, time, weather, and so on. The specialist then investigates differences in the data, utilizing the power of statistics. If conditions present when good products are made differ from conditions present when defective ones are produced, the specialist has found a clue. If necessary, he or she can collect more data to reconfirm this conclusion. If the differences discovered are related to quality, a cause responsible for dispersion has been found, and the specialist can formulate methods to stabilize conditions. Once this is done, dispersion will diminish.

I am not suggesting that knowledge of proper manufacturing techniques is useless but that its usefulness is limited to providing hints and clues. The right measure to take can only be discovered through and confirmed by the data. *Everything* must be screened through data.

Once we master this point, we need not confine our activities to manufacturing processes. We can solve problems just as effectively in development, marketing, finance, or labor, so long as we observe the appropriate sequence of steps. In the next chapter, I will discuss this sequence.

CHAPTER | 7

Methods of Problem Solving

How to Hold a Brainstorming Session

The first step in eliminating defective products is to identify
what must be investigated. To do this, we call a meeting of
all the people who know something about the problem and ask
them what they think is causing defects and whether they have
seen anything unusual. Our memory is a remarkable mechanism, and the purpose of the meeting is to extract from it everything that might be relevant. To succeed in this, however, we
have to use a little strategy.

Whoever chairs the meeting will record every suggestion
made on a blackboard or notepad, in plain view. As people see
what is being written down, they remember other things they
had forgotten.

This process is called free association. It is important to remember that at this stage we are not trying to solve the problem
but simply to find clues. The proper atmosphere can help us a
great deal to get these clues. Everyone must feel free to speak
up. Often it's better to be informal and free wheeling, so people
are not afraid to say whatever comes to mind. If they expect to
be contradicted not much participation is likely. So spend a little extra time and have more than one meeting, if necessary. If
people want to smoke, let them; when they get tired, have a cof-
fee break.

These meetings perform a very important function — they give everyone the sense of working together to solve the problem. For this reason, an unassertive person may be better suited to chair the meeting; someone with strong opinions is likely to create some resentment and may be suspected of trying to lead the group toward a particular conclusion.

When everyone speaks freely, dozens of different opinions may be presented. The next step is to create a diagram that groups similar opinions together. Create categories for these groups, such as "problems related to materials," "design problems," "problems concerning workers," and so on. Then use these categories to create a new diagram and watch as new opinions begin to emerge.

One way of summarizing the opinions is to combine them in a cause-and-effect diagram affectionately known as the "fishbone" diagram. (See Figure 9.) This is a favorite of QC consultants, but you need not feel bound to it. It has often been used successfully, however, so I would recommend it to those who are just starting QC.

Analyzing Past Data (Stratification)

A cause-and-effect diagram organizes everything people have observed about a certain problem. This does not mean that the cause of product defects will become immediately obvious. The diagram simply lines up all the potential culprits. To know what really caused the problem requires proof.

Our method is very simple. All we know is this: Something in the manufacturing process changed at some point and we are getting different results. So we begin by analyzing all the data available on the conditions that may cause defects.

Pick any factor that varies, group all the available data, and compare the average defect rates for each group. For example, let's say that the weather conditions have been recorded. Group the working days into two categories, clear days and rainy days. Add up defect rates on the clear days and compute

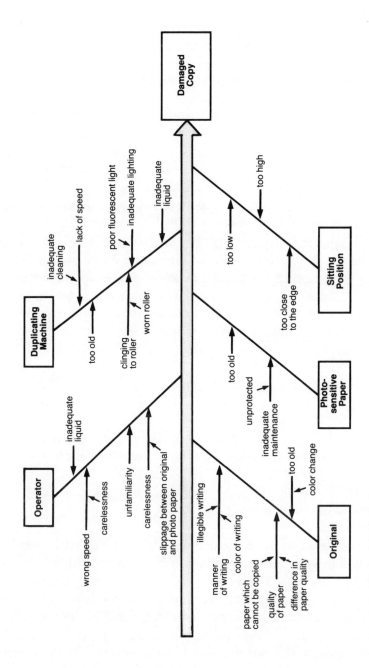

Figure 9. Cause and Effect Diagram

their mean value. Then do likewise for the rainy days. If the two mean values differ, you should consider the possibility that the weather affected the results. If there is no discrepancy, you need not investigate further.

Similarly in the factory, use as headings any factors that help you distinguish between groups of data. Group the data under those headings and compare mean values. You can use any factors on which records have been kept, for example, lot numbers of materials, names of workers, days of the week or times of manufacture, distinctive marks made by the equipment, serial numbers of jigs, and so on. Study the differences between them through the data, one by one, even if there seems to be no reason to suspect any of being contributing factors.

We engage in this process because we can learn a lot from past data. We try to arrive at the point where what we can learn from the past ends and the unknown begins — then we stop. It takes time and money to obtain new data which makes using past data a cost-effective method. Moreover, this analysis of past data can give us clues for future study, so we pursue it thoroughly.

The key to using this method successfully is the same as in crime detection. Both situations require that we immerse ourselves in general knowledge which then serves as a base for future activity. We build this base in the factory by firmly establishing in our minds all the conditions of the manufacturing process. Thorough investigation of past data is the important first step.

Method of Observation

As a result of the brainstorming session, you will probably have many potential candidates for the cause of defects. As I pointed out in the last section, the next step is to get supporting evidence by investigating every possible piece of recorded data you can find. Usually, much can be uncovered in this way; then, however, you must visit the actual workplace. As the ancients said, "One visit is worth a thousand words." Unlike the information in graphs and numbers which is abstract, the data we obtain on a visit to the actual workplace is direct and complete.

The *way* you observe, however, can make a great deal of difference. Obviously, if you inspect the workplace absentmindedly you will not see anything meaningful. What, then, are the strategies for success? Here are a few pointers:

First, look for something no one has mentioned before, perhaps something no one has even noticed. This is not as difficult as it may sound. People usually have a preconceived idea about what the real cause is, but if we could depend on what people *think*, most problems would have been solved long ago. In fact, I've said this before, but it bears repeating: The cause that springs to mind easily is rarely the true one — that's why the problem is still around.

Next, look for anything that varies from a normal pattern. If you see any deviation from what is expected, consider it a possible cause and investigate it thoroughly.

These are the two most important strategies for making meaningful observations. Now let's look at some examples.

Strategy 1: Finding the Culprit in an Unlikely Place

At a light bulb factory, the study of quality control was begun in earnest to qualify for the Japan Industrial Standard (JIS) mark. [Editor's note: It is similar to the Underwriter's Laboratory (UL) mark.] When factory personnel began drawing up control charts, they encountered some difficulty. Of all the characteristics of a light bulb, the most important is efficiency, which is defined as the ratio of brightness to amount of electricity consumed. This ratio almost always varied widely from bulb to bulb, exceeding the control limits. To improve efficiency, the factory collected data on every conceivable cause and then analyzed the data. One year passed without conclusive results. As the day of inspection for JIS neared, the factory management approached me for advice.

When I visited the factory, data on all processes had been carefully collected for a one-year period so I had nothing to do in that regard. I began with a study of materials, comparing my data with the study that had already been done, point by point. I was impressed by the meticulous way they had carried out all aspects of the study. However, at the last moment, I noticed something odd that occurred when the finished light bulb's efficiency was monitored. Two inspectors carried out this task with a precision measuring instrument. When taking the measurement, they lowered the sensitivity setting. I asked them why they did not raise the sensitivity level, and they told me that whenever they did, the needle on the instrument became unstable and difficult to read.

The same thing happened when I tried: When I raised the sensitivity level, the needle in the meter became unstable. Thinking this was a case of a poor contact, I had the instrument and everything else thoroughly cleaned, but there was no change. I looked into the spherical instrument that is used to measure the brightness of a bulb. Inside it, the bulb's brightness seemed to flicker. I brought in a voltmeter, measured the voltage and found that it fluctuated. When I lit the bulb with a battery, however, the needle on the instrument held steady at one point. Even when the measuring instrument was set at the highest sensitivity, the needle showed accurate values.

The control charts had in effect been recording not the brightness of the light bulbs, but the voltage of the power source. I asked if they had a constant-voltage regulator, and they said they did. When I examined it, I found a switching device that was activated when the voltage changed. A motor began to turn, and the voltage changed slowly. With a device like this, there was no chance of responding to the constant voltage changes. The chart showed voltage as constant, and no one had bothered to check the actual operation of the regulator. To ensure that the test results would not be influenced by temporary disruptions in the voltage supply, I had the device replaced with a more sensitive instrument that could respond to even the smallest changes in voltage. Once this was done, we discovered that there was actually very little variation between light bulbs. Our problem was solved.

Strategy 2: The Secret of Observation

The second strategy is to investigate thoroughly any conditions that appear unusual. This means discovering every dispersion, that is, every possible deviation from normal patterns.

Is there a difference in the units between those produced in the morning and those produced in the afternoon? If a piece of equipment is placed near a window or in the middle of the shop, will results differ? How about differences between the work done a day after a holiday versus two days after a holiday? Detailed information, such as difference between workers and differences in the finish of raw materials, must be studied carefully to determine whether it affects the dispersion in quality in any way.

This careful attention to detail is the key to successful observation. Once our QC activities have come this far, they are much like crime detection. But unlike crime detectives, we condition ourselves to look at things through the perspective of dispersion. QC practitioners are trained that way.

Once you get used to this work, it is not especially difficult to discover clues for the cause of defects just by wandering around the factory. Sometimes you can discover what is wrong just by closing your eyes and listening to the sounds. If the machines hum at about the same pitch, there is probably no problem. At times, however, you can hear dissonance — the screeching or sharp ear-splitting sounds that always indicate a problem.

Once I observed a problem on the assembly line at a bulldozer factory. A bulldozer has two caterpillars, continuous metal tracks that run along each side. To assemble these caterpillars, one worker inserted bolts on one side of the assembly line, while a worker on the opposite side tightened the bolts by screwing on nuts. There were always some nuts that were screwed on too tightly.

Workers used wrenches, and normally the nuts tightened without any trouble. But one or two in ten did not fit snugly. Sometimes a single twist of the wrench sufficed, while at other times it was a struggle to tighten the nut. The pattern was definitely abnormal. And where there is dispersion, there is room for improvement.

I examined the nuts that were difficult to tighten and discovered that the screw threads on some of the bolts were damaged; they looked as though they had struck something. Production of these bolts had been subcontracted, and I could not believe that a subcontractor would submit such defective parts.

Further investigation revealed that the cause was a simple one. The company inspected the bolts on delivery by taking a few from each box. After inspection, these bolts were carelessly thrown back into the boxes from which they had been taken. As the hexagonal head of the bolt struck and rolled over the other bolts in the box, it damaged their screw threads. The company unwittingly created defective bolts in the very process of inspecting them!

We immediately told the inspectors to handle the bolts more carefully. By the next day none of the bolts were difficult to tighten. This single measure increased efficiency by 15 percent.

Keep Records

When the factory is very large, it takes time to observe the entire workplace, so you must keep accurate records. When you decide to keep records, however, you must collect data thoroughly. Halfhearted data-gathering creates problems for you later on.

In the old days, when a convict escaped into the hills, townspeople were mobilized into search parties. They were each given an area about one meter in width and told to comb the hills thoroughly side by side. This might be hard to do in a modern factory, but considering all the trouble defects can cause, it is wise to mobilize as many people as possible to help track down the causes of future problems.

Mobilizing the workers is easier said than done, however. As an alternative, look for ways to gather the data automatically. For example, give inspectors a tape recorder each and ask them to record a detailed description of defects as soon as they find them.

I have already talked about the method of analyzing past data. Keeping thorough records insures that we can use this same method in the future without having to collect a lot of historical data first.

At a factory producing thin steel plate, deviation in the thickness of the product could not be reduced below a certain value no matter what measures were taken.

Although it was quite time consuming, we decided to examine the finished products one by one. We measured the thickness of the plate at five-centimeter intervals and constructed a graph. This graph (Figure 10) shows that the thickness of the plate changed slightly with obvious regularity. After a lengthy search we found that the wave form corresponded to one of the many rollers used in the process that was defective. As soon as we replaced it with a new one, our problem was solved.

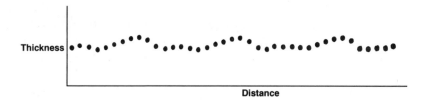

Figure 10.

Experimentation

The final secret is: *test it yourself*. Change the conditions governing a factor that you suspect is causing the defects, and see if the results are different. In other words — experiment.

For example, if you are not sure whether the temperature of the plating solution is right, deliberately raise or lower it and start plating. Then compare results.

There is one rule, however, that you must follow when you experiment in the factory and that is to set a reasonable range for your experimentation. If you decide to vary the temperature in the plating solution, for example, the range must be within the upper and lower limits of the established standard. Your experimentation must begin at the mean value. The reason for this is simple: if work standards have been set, the acceptable temperature range for the plating solution has already been determined. If you go outside the range, you will only create additional defects and the result will contribute little or nothing to a better grasp of conditions.

Factory Experimentation

This kind of experimentation is called *factory experimentation*. If we are not confident that the raw materials currently used are suitable, we can change them and watch what happens. Similarly, we can have different workers perform a certain task or change the speed of processing. In this manner, we eventually find the most suitable combination.

For example, assume that the specification for the thickness of a steel plate is 1.2 mm ± 0.1 mm. For your factory experiment, select three different thicknesses to test: the first, 1.1 mm thick, the thinnest plate acceptable under the specification; a second, 1.3 mm thick, which is the thickest acceptable plate; and the third, 1.2 mm thick, a middle value. When the steel plates are delivered, measure their thickness with a micrometer or slide calipers. Using felt-tipped markers, mark the three different thicknesses with different colors. Then put the plates through the actual manufacturing process in random order. Study the finished products to determine if there is any difference in the defective rate by color of steel plate.

Thus, another way to discover causes of defects is to test the specifications and work standards currently in use. We are often perplexed when materials that meet our specifications produce defective parts, or when well trained, experienced workers produce final products that are below standard. So look carefully at your standards and don't experiment with materials that do not meet your specifications. If you do, don't be surprised when defects are produced.

When you carry out experiments in a laboratory, it's easy to create ideal conditions. For example, if pure water is necessary to achieve certain results, all a scientist has to do to get perfect results is to remove all impurities from the water. In laboratory experimentation, conditions can be modified to create optimal environments.

In manufacturing, however, you must work with the materials, the manufacturing facilities, and the workers that are available in the workplace. Furthermore, costs must be minimized which makes it impossible to create the optimal environment in which all the factors that may have an adverse effect on quality have been eliminated. At times, the negligence of subcontractors may cause damage during transport; another time your emergency use of inexperienced part-time workers may be the cause.

Fortunately, the degree of contribution differs greatly for each factor influencing quality. One item may appear to have the greatest impact, until further investigation shows that another factor contributes far more to the problem.

So try to gather and analyze as much concrete data as possible on every conceivable factor. Once this is done, it will become clear which factor is influencing the situation and in what way. If initial data are insufficient, you can supplement them later on. If there is a difference in mean values, it will become clearer through this process. This is yet another application of the law of large numbers.

Quality control succeeds because it quantifies cause-and-effect relationships statistically. By using statistical methods we can discover correlations we never thought existed, especially conditions that may have escaped our notice when viewed exclusively from our technological perspective.

The relationship between the tuner and speaker mentioned in Chapter 6 illustrates this point very well. Once we are able to pinpoint that relationship through data, the engineers may be in a position to find a scientific explanation of the cause-and-effect relationship. That knowledge is always acquired after the fact, however; it cannot be found through theoretical speculation alone.

Production Is Always an Experiment

Remember that when we experiment, even though we may not uncover the causes of defects, we can begin to eliminate them. Science can tell us precisely how, for example, a magnet attracts a piece of steel. Even without understanding the way it works, however, we can learn how to use the magnet simply by observing it.

Good products are developed through experimentation. Master craftsmen are people who manage to find the best ways of making things. As long as their craft remains a secret, however, it cannot become the basis of an industry. Quality control can be viewed as a way of teaching these methods to everyone, using the science of statistics.

Ultimately, experience is the real "statistics." As a discipline, it provides a way to discover regularity or patterns in massive amounts of seemingly heterogeneous data. Similarly, workers gain experience or skill through repetition in their work. If their work were different from day to day there could be no accumulation of experience.

Thus our daily production activities can be thought of as experiments, the cost of which, incidentally, is borne by our customers. Since we are already conducting many experiments at no extra cost, it should not be too difficult to find out in the process what is good for quality, provided we collect adequate data. Here are two things to keep in mind:

Gather accurate data and preserve them. In manufacturing we receive materials which we then inspect, process, assemble, package, and finally ship as finished products. Without records we won't be able to tell how these products were made at a later date. Do not be complacent. In each area good experiments are going on all the time — utilize them to the fullest extent possible by recording the processes and methods employed.

Know how to analyze these data. Methods are needed to find regular patterns in the mountains of data. If you find precious stones in the mountains but don't know how to cut them, all you have is a pile of pebbles. Statistical quality control provides methodical procedures that everyone can use. I have emphasized the need to calculate mean values, but this is the simplest possible method — merely the first step. There are many more sophisticated methods; master them, and you will begin to make some startling discoveries.

So, What if You Can't Experiment with Weather?

Experiments do work outside the laboratory and can be just as effective in manufacturing plants. Experiments alone, however, will not show us the impact of something that is beyond human control.

The weather is a good example. If we need a clear day for an experiment, it's just too bad if the weather doesn't cooperate — there's nothing we can do about it. Yet we cannot completely disregard the impact the weather may have on all our activities.

This means that we must keep a meticulous record of all the factors we suspect of being causes and investigate the results. Once enough data have been accumulated, we can group the data in categories by the conditions governing the causes and then compute the mean values of the results for comparison.

We can accumulate data on the weather, for example, for a period of one to two months, separate them into data for clear days versus rainy days, add up the defect rates for the clear days, and then compute the mean value. We can then do the same thing for the rainy days and compare the two mean values. Assuming that the mean value for defective rates on clear days is

2.1 percent and for rainy day 8.5 percent, we can reasonably infer that weather is a contributing factor because of such a wide spread between mean values. Before rendering a final judg-ment, we might want to do some more investigating, but we have at least obtained some valuable clues.

In this example, a large amount of data must be gathered to make a comparison. There will be clear days when the defect rate may be higher and rainy days when it is actually lower. If weather is believed to be a contributing factor, however, you must accumulate a large amount of data and compute mean values. Regardless of the differences from day to day, there is bound to be a spread that confirms the observation. Once again, this is an application of the law of large numbers.

Quality control uses statistics like a net to pull in potential causes of defects and provide valuable clues. Nothing can match the usefulness of data.

CHAPTER | 8

Statistics

Statistical Analysis

Many people associate statistics with difficult mathematics. This may be the result of schools not teaching the subject properly, because once you know something about statistics, you realize that it is mostly common sense. Or, to put it differently, common sense is a kind of statistics.

We tend to think of Scandinavians as tall people, for example, but not all Scandinavians are tall. If we gather data on the height of a great many Scandinavians and compute a mean value, however, we find that on the average, they are certainly taller than the Japanese.

To see a trend, we cannot compare individuals one by one; we must look at many people. If we do so, our conclusions have some universality. That's what common sense amounts to: deriving principles from repeated observation.

Actually, historical data tell us that Scandinavians have not always been so tall. In the early part of the Meiji era (around the 1870s), the average Scandinavian was no taller than the average Japanese. So what is it that caused Scandinavians to increase in size since then? One contributing factor has been their eating habits, which changed to include more animal protein.

Since the war, the Japanese have also been eating differently and growing taller on a Westernized diet that includes butter and milk. We have observed the correlation between eating habits and height through data on the Scandinavians; now the Japanese are providing additional support for that statistical correlation.

Here again, we may not have a scientific explanation for how changes in eating habits affect the growth mechanism, but we can use the information without that knowledge. An individual's height is determined by heredity and living conditions, along with an almost limitless range of additional factors that interact to cause him or her to grow to a certain height. It is virtually impossible to discover any correlation between height and eating habits when we look at people individually. But once we obtain and compare the mean value from data accumulated on tens of thousands of people, a clear-cut trend does emerge.

We cannot always reason theoretically to a precise cause-and-effect relationship, so we look to the statistics. If we find a correlation, we can make inferences based on the numbers at our disposal. This is a very potent tool in any area of manufacturing.

One Method of Determining Design

Items such as radios, wristwatches, and women's shoes have one thing in common: They compete in terms of design while they may not differ in quality or function. All three are, in some sense, fashion products and therefore involve considerable design effort.

When our designers continuously develop new and attractive ideas, how do we choose which one to produce? The loudest voice or the most persistent salesperson often wins out, unfortunately.

To address this problem, a watchmaker decided to compile data by asking all his employees to give their opinion on each new design. Each employee voted on the design and wrote his or her name on the ballot.

At first, when a new design was introduced on the market, the company soon knew by the volume of sales whether or not it had a hit with the public. To avoid introducing unpopular designs, the following approach was instituted: Using the ballots, the company separated employees into two groups — those whose answers were consistent with public opinion and those who were not. Over time, the company was able to identify those employees who consistently showed good design sense, that is, the ones whose votes were consistent with subsequent public response. These employees were then separated into sub-groups of those particularly adept at modern design, those accurate as to luxury items, and so on. Once this list was complete, the company had a winning formula: the next style of watch in a given category could be selected by those who had accurately predicted good design in the past.

We do not know why some people have a better design sense than others; it hardly matters, though, because they are useful to the company even if we don't understand how and why. Naturally, the individuals used to predict popular designs were not told about the role they played; otherwise they might have become self-conscious. And, if the company had undertaken a study of psychological profiles and shown the results to the employees concerned, their good sense might even have been destroyed.

In Japanese we refer to this sixth sense as "*kan.*" In our example, the company was able to provide the *kan* of its employees with a scientific base through the statistical method.

Useful and Useless Data

You may conclude, based on the previous example, that collecting and analyzing this sort of market data will pay rich dividends for your company. One well-known Japanese executive, however, insists that such surveys are useless. According to Soichiro Honda, "Market surveys, like the psychology of a woman, are quite unreliable." Needless to say, he may find himself in hot water with an argument like that, but there are in fact many market surveys that are quite useless. Why is this so? There are basically two reasons.

First, people often study something that is useless to begin with. You cannot study meaningless data and expect to reach a useful conclusion. Data are merely shadows of reality, and shadows change their shape as the location of the light source changes. Many surveys seem to have been done by light from strange directions.

If the light comes from the wrong direction, it may be impossible to deduce the reality from the shadow it casts. For example, when light shines on a round tray from a source right beside it, the shadow produced is a straight line. To conclude correctly from this straight line that the tray is round would be pure guesswork, without any real foundation. As this example illustrates, the first condition in obtaining data is to know what direction the light is coming from, in other words, what we are gathering data about.

This principle applies not only to market surveys but also to data for controlling manufacturing processes, inspection data, and data relating to labor and finance. Unless we know what they really mean, we will collect data that lead to poor decisions.

Secondly, data can become useless in other ways. For example, we may gather correct data but make mistakes when drawing conclusions. The following is one of my favorite examples; you can think of it as a parable if you wish.

Two Salesmen

After World War I, a large number of Japanese salesmen descended on Saipan and other islands in the Pacific, former German protectorates that had become Japanese mandated territories.

One day two shoe salesmen arrived on one of these islands. Shortly after their arrival, they sent their reports back to Tokyo. The first salesman wrote, "The natives here all go barefoot, so there is no demand for shoes and no prospect of making a sale."

The second salesman wrote differently: "As soon as I arrived, I realized that we have a golden opportunity here. All the natives are barefoot. If all these people were to start wearing shoes, it would create an enormous demand. This is the most promising market I have found."

The two saw precisely the same condition, but their conclusions were completely opposite. One thought there would be no demand, while the other saw the chance for a highly promising market. Why was there such a great difference?

The report of the first salesman was certainly persuasive. It contained no logical contradiction, and the data backed his assertion. His report was worthless for the shoe manufacturer, however. How so? A survey that merely describes the present condition is of no use. The salesman had been sent to the island to sell shoes. So in his survey, his objective should have been to find ways of selling shoes. Observing everything from this standpoint he could then collect suitable data.

The second salesman did try to see whether shoes could be sold on the island. He probably let people try on his samples. He might even have determined which types of shoes would suit the natives. Of course, data on prices that would be appropriate for this market would also have been useful, as well as information on potential wholesalers and what the profit margin would be.

In short, a survey to find out how to sell shoes is quite different from a survey to identify potential customers. If you study something useless, there is no way you'll ever get useful results.

Data for Action

If objectives differ, so will the subject matter to be investigated and the manner in which conclusions are obtained. This principle also holds true when collecting data for technological improvement.

When defective products appear, engineers collect various data and use them to explain why they were produced. But no matter how often a QC engineer tells the workers *why* defective products were produced, the number of defects will not diminish. The real issue is *how* to reduce these defects. For this, a method must be found and action taken.

The way data are collected will be quite different if the original objective is to find out *how* to reduce defects rather than *why* they occur.

Assume that temperature has an effect on the defect rate. If our only interest is to find the cause, we may want to keep an accurate record of temperatures. If we are gathering data in order to lower the defect rate, however, we may want to study how the dial or valve is turned in adjusting the temperature; we may look at the material and how much is used in a particular operation; we may also study the steps of that operation. In this instance, even if we know what the ideal temperature is, we still must determine how to set the dial accurately to reach that ideal temperature. We must also confirm that this condition can be duplicated.

Unfortunately, there are many engineers and technicians who are as shortsighted about the need to gather data for problem solving as the first shoe salesman was about the islanders' demand for shoes. This difference in objective is a basic difference between research conducted in a laboratory and the factory. It lies in how we think about problems, and this basic attitude must be instilled in everyone connected with QC activities. To these people I want to emphasize that quality control is not a discipline that *explains* but one that *solves* problems.

When we collect data, we must collect it *for the purpose of solving problems*. In other words, we need data for action. We do not collect data merely to gain knowledge, at least not in manufacturing plants.

Chance versus Probability

Quality control is characterized by its dedication to fact control, the goal of making judgments based on factual data through statistics.

In the real world, certain events happen accidentally, while others are caused. Suppose someone found $500,000 on the sidewalk in a shopping center. This sort of thing rarely happens, and when it does it's by chance.

In contrast, some events are inevitable; they happen for a reason, and if you watch long enough you will witness them. Statistics helps us distinguish between what happens by *chance* and what happens for a reason, that is, what is likely or *probable*.

When defective products are produced, we use statistics to differentiate between those occurring accidentally and those that were highly likely to occur. Then we take steps to assure that the conditions creating the predictable defects do not recur. This idea — distinguishing chance events from predictable ones and taking steps to prevent the latter — is the principle behind statistical quality control.

That is why specialists in quality control must also be experts in statistics. Because they must use whatever tools are available for problem solving, there is no limit to the amount of statistical analysis demanded of them. The Japanese Union of Scientists and Engineers (JUSE) has developed a basic training program for QC staff. This program enjoys an excellent reputation and its graduates are regarded by many as the mainstay of Japan's entire QC movement. The first lecture in the series on statistics and mathematics covers data collection methods. Other topics are those shown in Table 6.

For the student who completes this program, there are additional specialized courses in experimental design, calculus of several variables, market surveying, reliability engineering, operations research, and industrial engineering. Basic knowledge of computer programming is essential for successful completion of these courses.

While the QC specialist must become familiar with many disciplines, it is not a matter of rote memorization. His or her purpose is to acquire skills that will facilitate problem solving which makes the learning process surprisingly easy.

A word of caution: Those who take courses like these should not become overly absorbed in the collection of data for their

Analyzing Data
Probability and Statistics
Testing and Inference
Testing and Inferring by Variable
Testing and Inferring by Attribute
Control Charts
Sampling Inspection
Scatter Analysis
Correlation Analysis
Simple Analysis
Orthogonal Analysis
Binomial Probability
Linear Algebra
Regression and Regression Analysis
Sampling
Work Sampling
Reliability Engineering
Optimization Method
Sensory Inspection
Design of Experiment

Table 6: JUSE Quality Control Curriculum

own sake, no matter how interesting. It is important to remember that data are just data, collected to help us distinguish
chance events from predictable outcomes for the purpose of solving problems.

CHAPTER 9

Total Quality Control

TQC

Many quality control methods have been developed to eliminate defects. These methods had to be simple so that
anyone could learn to use them. Once learned, however, it
would be a shame to restrict their application to product quality. As I mentioned earlier, quality control specialists like to
tackle problems associated with any variety of product —
metal materials, automobiles, rubber tires. They can and do
succeed in all these areas. As a production manager at the
Japan Broadcasting Company (NHK) once said, quality control is a discipline dedicated to problem solving.

Companies that have successfully introduced quality control
in one or two divisions often get good results when they apply
similar methods in their other divisions. In other words, quality
assurance is a company wide problem that often cannot be
solved by the manufacturing divisions alone. Many different
issues come up, so QC's gradual penetration into other depart-
ments is natural.

No matter how much effort is made in manufacturing, defective parts and products cannot be eliminated when designs are
faulty. When we search for causes, we often discover that slight
changes in design can totally eliminate the defects. Thus, quality

control is indispensable in the area of design. This is also essential in purchasing. If a company purchases poorly made products, the factory can do nothing about it. Selecting reliable vendors and knowing how to make purchases are important considerations.

How workers are hired and assigned to jobs also has a direct bearing on quality control; so does adequacy of facilities. Marketing and other sales activities and service are very important as well, as is the backing of a strong sales force if a factory is to engage in production at stable levels. Conversely, if the production plan fluctuates constantly, the sales force will be hard pressed to align sales with production. In quality control, customer complaints provide an important source of information. Finally, no quality control specialist can forget the importance of cost.

The idea of total quality control (TQC) grew out of concerns such as these. Initially, other divisions had a lot of resistance to implementing it. Quality control people, they felt, should stay in the factories and do their jobs there, not interfere in management or personnel matters.

However, quality problems arise from the nature of the company itself (*kōgyō taishitsu*) and are inseparable from the company as a whole. Certainly, management is the same thing as quality control; to make quality control a success, however, the entire company must strive for quality. Looked at this way, the success or failure of quality control clearly depends on the attitude and support of top management.

TQC as a Management Policy

When we look for examples of successful quality control in Japan, we discover that only those companies have been successful that are led by presidents who acknowledge the importance of quality control and implement it throughout the organization. It is this approach, ultimately, that creates profits and satisfied customers and provides a stable foundation for company management.

Theoretically everyone knows that it is best to sell a good product; there is no better policy for a company than to make a sincere commitment to producing quality products. But is this carried out in practice? There have always been doubters. After the first oil crisis, however, Japanese companies experienced a prolonged period of unspectacular but stable growth. This period proved the theory's validity, since Japanese firms were well established in the practice of selling high quality merchandise.

In a period of high growth, companies can make minor mistakes without their growth or profits being significantly affected. A period of stable growth, however, reveals which products are really good. Customers become much more discriminating and buy only high quality products. This trend has been observed worldwide and has made Japanese products even more desirable. Fortunately, Japan's industries were prepared for this contingency even before the oil crisis.

Looking at the economy in this way, we can appreciate the importance of making TQC a company wide policy. TQC is a distinct management strategy. Unless it guides every employee's thinking, TQC cannot succeed. Once it gains full acceptance, however, TQC will strengthen a company enormously.

Many people in the West and in developing countries insist that the responsibility for quality in manufacturing rests with specialists. To produce excellent products and supply them to customers, however, requires that everyone pitch in with his or her best effort. This effort begins with formulation of quality goals, followed by development of designs, a purchasing policy for raw materials and parts, control methods for manufacturing processes, improvement activities, and sales and service activities. Nothing can be left out. Considered separately, these activities seem quite specialized, but they all need a principled core around which to succeed — TQC.

Today, as TQC's reputation grows, even companies in non-manufacturing fields are adopting it. In these companies as in manufacturing, individual workers participate in a company-wide effort and are given the will to succeed by top management support.

Quality Assurance Is a Job for the Entire Company

When a customer complains, the first reaction is to blame the people who inspected the merchandise. "Why did you overlook these defects?" they may be asked. The inspectors are then ordered to give more thought to their inspection activities and perform them more carefully.

There is some merit in this approach which stems from the notion that manufacturers should be responsible for finding and discarding defective products. Of course, only perfect products should be supplied to the marketplace; and if this simple principle were observed, there would be no defective units. It is, however, an old-fashioned and simplistic approach to the problem.

Actually, when we think of the quality of a product, we have many things in mind. Consider a watch, for example. We can inspect some aspects of quality directly: Does it keep accurate time? Does it have scratches on the housing? But inspection cannot answer questions about how long the watch will run or how frequently it will break down. A lengthy endurance test will tell us this, but we receive the information only when the watch breaks down. In the case of a watch, we can affirm quality without being able to assure it.

If a restaurant owner insists on inspecting every dish and drink in his establishment, nothing can be sold. Similarly, film that has been exposed during inspection cannot be used again.

Actually, only a limited number of quality characteristics can be inspected. So, from the standpoint of economics, when inspection cost is several times that of manufacturing cost, something is inherently wrong. In such a situation, it is better to select a few samples from a batch of the same product and inspect them. If you have a sample watch that has run more than 10 years, you can infer that other watches made the same way will also last ten years. This is the logic behind the method of inspection sampling.

The quality of our watch is thus assured by obtaining information on how the watch was made and what its durability is. Generally, a product's quality may be judged by examining the following five characteristics:

1. *Engineering principles.* On what technological principles are design and manufacturing based?

2. *Design.* Is the design sound? No matter how excellent the engineering principles of a product may be, if the design is poor, the quality will be poor.

3. *Manufacturing conditions.* Under what factory conditions is the item produced? How is the manufacturing process managed?

4. *Inspection data.* Bearing in mind that not every individual item is inspected, what information about the product can be gathered through inspection?

5. *Data on actual use.* How does the product perform when it is used by the customer?

Obviously, if quality is measured from all of these perspectives, it cannot be assured through manufacturing and inspection alone. Quality assurance has really always been the responsibility of the entire company.

Suppliers Must Also Engage in QC

When visiting factories outside Japan, I still meet people who insist that quality control can be delegated to specialists in the field or performed exclusively through inspection.

If a manufacturing process produces poor products, the quality of the product cannot be trusted, no matter how thoroughly it is inspected. As I have said many times, quality control means that we stop producing defective parts and products. On the other hand, when the defect rate reaches zero, inspection is no longer necessary. When you cannot find a single defect through inspection, no matter how hard you try, it becomes a waste of time. The ultimate goal of quality control, then, is to abolish the inspection office!

You can use the same approach toward suppliers. Even the most stringent inspection at the receiving end cannot completely prevent delivery of defective parts or materials with the good ones. Whenever this happens you may have to rework subassemblies; you may also face additional customer complaints.

Instead of wasting effort on trying to improve receiving inspection, it would be better to require that your suppliers engage in quality control as well, so that you can eliminate this costly practice.

It is extremely important to select good suppliers. If they are concerned only with delivering goods and getting paid on time, they are likely to think that supplying defective parts is acceptable because they can always be replaced. Whenever materials and parts must be replaced, however, delivery dates are delayed. It may even cause confusion in your own manufacturing cycles — a condition diametrically opposed to that sought through Toyota's kanban and just-in-time methods.

Unless you select suppliers who are dedicated to reaching zero defects, you can expect trouble for yourself in the future. To become a manufacturer of high-quality products, you must require dedication to quality control from all your suppliers and from any other companies with whom you do business.

We can set aside theories for examples. Look at any of the Japanese companies that are successful in quality control — not one of them engages in quality control without the full cooperation of their suppliers.

The Deming application prize is given to Japanese companies with a proven record of quality control. Quite a few medium- and small-sized enterprises have received this prize, many of them parts manufacturers. This indirectly confirms that a company's pursuit of quality control requires the cooperation of every one of its subcontractors.

The High Level of Quality Control Japanese-Style

Quality control was born in the United States. In the 1920s, Dr. W.A. Shewhart, an American engineer, invented statistical quality control. Japan adopted it completely following

World War II. Initially it was a transplanted American system, but gradually quality control began to take on uniquely Japanese characteristics.

Even in ancient times, the Japanese were known to possess a genius for absorbing knowledge from abroad. Pictographic Chinese characters (*kanji*) were imported from China and used to create a set of peculiarly Japanese phonetic symbols called *kana*. Today, both *kanji* and *kana* characters are used in the Japanese writing system. Similarly, the Japanese have been able to adapt quality control to answer the needs of their industries and create a system unique to Japan.

In Japanese, this system is called *hinshitsu kanri*, which in English means "quality control." Initially, "quality" meant quality of product. However, as we gain more and more experience in quality control, we are discovering that quality is not confined to products. There are characteristics of quality in every field of work that can be controlled — for example, quality of performance in both office work and sales. Japanese successes in these various areas have been quite extraordinary.

As quality control was adapted to Japanese business and Japanese labor-management relations, we developed QC circle activities, something that had not been done anywhere else. Today Japanese-style TQC is considered a unique system the world over and business managers in America and other countries want to re-import it to their own countries.

In the past decade, Japanese export products have been known for their high quality; but high quality is not limited to goods manufactured for export. If improvements in quality were confined to only one sector, the reputation of Japanese products in general would not have improved as much as it has. This achievement was possible only because quality in all areas went up — in machining processes, raw materials, assembly, and all other areas of manufacturing.

When a product is created, every step relating to its production must be placed under quality control. Otherwise, there is no way to assure high-quality. Similarly, Japanese products generally cannot be considered high quality if only some of them exhibit good qualities.

Behind the reputation of Japanese products lies the high level of quality control achieved by many Japanese companies. The success of quality control in Japan is not something attained by just one company or industry. It is the result of a general improvement in the level of TQC, industry-wide, in most areas.

Two Million Quality Control Specialists

A great deal of effort is required to abolish an inspection section or cut out receiving inspection. When nothing is going right, the first sign is an increase in the defect rate. Later, you will see it in increases in cost or in the number of breakdowns after sales, as well as in customer complaints. All these problems must be isolated, documented, and solved.

In quality control, moreover, there is no substitute for achieving a perfect grade of 100, a 99 just won't do. A single, small slip-up somewhere can result in hidden defects. No one is perfect, however, and everyone is bound to make mistakes. That is why we insist that everyone in the company help out with quality control.

Workers in the workplace often get blamed for inadequate design, defects in raw materials from suppliers, inappropriate work standards, inadequate control of equipment, and many other failures. But when all workers become attentive to conditions in the workplace, they can uncover every mistake imaginable, not just those for which they may be blamed.

QC circles were initially formed in the workplace for this very purpose. Everywhere QC was applied, workers expressed a desire to work together in the various improvement activities called for under quality control. The movement spread like wildfire throughout Japan. Today, there are probably more than two million people participating in QC circle activities.

Thus, quality control, born in the United States and imported to Japan, began to move in an entirely unexpected direction. As the reputation of Japanese products has grown, observers travel to Japan to see TQC in action for themselves. Without exception, these visitors are impressed by the commitment to quality control expressed and manifested all the way from top management to line workers.

When I tell these observers that more than two million people participate in QC circle activities, some of them draw the premature conclusion that TQC equals QC circle activities. That is of course not correct, so in the next chapter I will clarify the function of the QC circle.

CHAPTER | 10

QC Circles

The QC Circle Movement

The first international conference on quality control was held in Tokyo in 1969. Its program included visits to various factories, among them the car radio factory where I worked and welcomed a number of specialists from outside Japan. We presented actual examples of QC circle activities and then opened up the meeting for a question and answer period. One visitor asked us the following question:

> "The improvement activities you describe must be performed by engineers. It doesn't make sense for workers in the workplace to handle those activities. What is your opinion?"

I did not like the question. A worker who had made a presentation on QC circles gave the following answer:

> "I can understand why you say this. In our company, however, I'm the one who knows more about a particular process than anyone else. I was the one who suggested changes in the process when I discovered it was not running smoothly. My suggestions were adopted, and the defect rate decreased to one-third the previous figure. What could be wrong with my participating in these improvement activities?"

This answer accurately reflects the philosophy behind QC circles. Our visitor asked no further questions.

QC circles got their start when industry management realized that everyone's cooperation was necessary, especially that of the workers, if we wanted to create high-quality products. The Japanese QC circle movement began at the grassroots level in 1962. Although today it is widespread and even includes overseas groups, it started as a voluntary movement right in the workplace.

After a certain level of success had been achieved, some people began to criticize the movement, claiming that management was forcing workers to engage in circle activities. Not long ago, I read an article by a college professor promoting this argument in a prestigious economics journal. I immediately wrote to him asking if he had ever been to a QC conference and inviting him to attend one.

It was a hostile letter, I'm afraid, and I did not expect an answer. But the professor did write back and indicated that his knowledge of the workplace was largely theoretical. QC is not theory, however; it is a *practice*, a way of changing the workplace. To understand the spirit of the QC circle, one has to experience it firsthand.

More than two decades have passed since QC circles began, and the number of people involved is continuing to grow. People who worry about small issues in management theory do not understand what it means that more than two million Japanese are involved in QC circles. I hope that every industry will begin to participate in QC circle activities!

Small Improvements Add Up to Big Results

Some people mistakenly perceive improvements suggested by QC circles as insignificant when judged by the standards set by specialists. On the contrary, many of these improvements are made about aspects of manufacturing processes that specialists would never think to examine. Suggestions appear regularly and are thought out carefully. Over time, a number of such small improvements can lead to big results, as demonstrated by the following improvement activity reported at a recent QC circle conference.

A woman working for a camera manufacturer succeeded in eliminating the creation of scrap paper at the blueprint machines used in factories and offices. Every company has a waste paper basket next to the blueprint machine for paper scrapped due to poor exposures. How could this waste be reduced to zero?

This worker and her colleagues had watched carefully to see when scrap paper was produced and had discovered that, in most instances, it occurred when someone did a trial print run. The machine accepts originals on several different types of paper but cannot print clearly unless its speed is modified to suit the thickness of the original. Paper waste occurred every time machine adjustments were made.

Only a limited number of different types of paper were used in blueprinting. Through careful observation, the workers determined the best print speed for each type of original, recorded this information on an instruction sheet, and placed copies of it in plastic cases near each blueprint machine. Now, with instructions for optimal settings available for each type of blueprint, no one making copies has to do a trial run. The first copy is always perfect. The result: no paper waste.

This kind of idea is not often produced by engineers or college-educated white-collar workers. It is an improvement that can come only from workers, like those in this example who worked near the blueprint machine all year round.

Some simple improvements, like these, can be adopted directly by any company. And when the ripple effect extends throughout the company, the total improvement becomes immense.

Although not all improvements can be transferred to other companies immediately, participating in a QC conference and listening to presentations by other circles can be enlightening. The harder a circle works, the more it also wants to learn from the experiences and innovations of other circles.

QC circle activities have succeeded because of a system of mutual encouragement and exchange. Those selected to give presentations are encouraged to do even better. Circles doing well in company-wide presentations are given the opportunity to participate in regional QC circle conferences. And if they perform well there, the way is open to giving a presentation at a national conference.

Bring Back Craftsmanship

Improved customer service is a common goal in QC circles. Often, before selecting a focus for activities, circle members study the incidence of defects reported by consumers as well as conditions in other companies. When group members see their QC improvement activities as a way of serving customers better, they become more enthusiastic about them.

Modern control methods (establishing standard times, for example) can be traced to the work of Frederick W. Taylor and Frank B. Gilbreth on scientific management and time-motion. Taylor and Gilbreth made valuable contributions; unfortunately, their approach created a wide gulf between those who produce the goods and those who manage the organization. Their views on workers were simple: Workers need only perform their work in the prescribed manner and should not be concerned with whatever else happens in the workplace.

The attitude that "nothing matters as long as you do your job" can create adversarial relationships, however — not just with customers but also with those responsible for other processes on the line. Whenever something is defective or does not fit well, the responsibility is passed on to someone else. This attitude inevitably leads us to rely exclusively on inspection to eliminate defective parts and products.

Once this attitude is established, discovering defects becomes rather difficult and anyone collecting data on defects may be accused of "nitpicking" — criticizing other people's work unnecessarily.

QC circle activities, in contrast, re-focus attention on the original goal of manufacturing or creating services — serving the customer. When workers are conscious of customers' needs, their work becomes more meaningful. This is why QC circles are so effective in raising worker morale. Gathering data on defects serves the preceding process, the subsequent process, and in the end the customer. No one sees that kind of activity as nitpicking.

For workers who feel like they are on a treadmill all day, QC circle activities provide an opportunity to think and to be heard and to feel like an important member of the organization. They can witness how the manufacturing process is improved by their suggestions. This is the joy of working. Workers have a greater sense of self worth knowing that their work can serve customers. In that sense, QC circle activities represent a return to the days of craftsmanship or of handcrafted products.

QC Circles Are Not Limited to the Work Center

There are many ways to run QC circles. In manufacturing (where control activities begin), teams are formed in the work centers. Leaders are selected to organize these teams and obtain data on quality from the inspection section. Then each team meets separately to analyze the data, discuss possible causes of defects, and develop improvement plans.

When the QC circle movement began in manufacturing work centers, its contributions were impressive. Everyone could participate and make improvements. It did not take long for the movement to spread beyond the manufacturing sector.

No matter what a worker's job is, if it is performed well it will support the efforts of co-workers. At least in part because of their involvement in circle activities the feeling of solidarity among workers in Japanese companies is high. To them, quality control makes good sense.

In a given company, QC circles may start in manufacturing and then spread to other divisions, such as finance and sales. Eventually, circles are created even by receptionists and telephone operators. In these companies, themes for improvement will not be restricted to eliminating defects in manufactured goods. Here's what happened at one company:

Factory A had a huge dining room that could seat as many as 1,400 people at a time. The staff responsible for serving tea and clearing the tables saw QC circle activities going on in the manufacturing division and decided to have a circle of their own.

There were many themes to choose from, but their final choice brought about a result even they had not expected. Consumption of tea leaves decreased 50 percent.

The kitchen workers noticed that people tended to sit at the same table each day. They reasoned that if people sat at the same tables each day, the amount of tea consumed at a certain table would also probably be the same each day. Their investigation revealed that at some tables far less tea was consumed than at others. If people at table X drank less tea, the staff thought, why supply as much tea to it as to tables where more tea was regularly consumed? Using this approach, the staff supplied as much tea to each table as was indicated by past consumption patterns. To their amazement, they needed only half as many tea leaves as previously used.

As this example demonstrates, QC circle activities are not limited to certain work centers or themes. Whatever the workplace or the job, there is quality that can be imparted to the work. The goal of QC circles is to improve this quality.

QC Circles Are Not Limited to Manufacturing

QC circle activities spread beyond the manufacturing sector and showed their effectiveness in activities for office workers, even telephone operators. Companies that did not own manufacturing facilities began to feel that QC activities were right for them, too.

Today, QC circle activities are being introduced in many different industries and companies in Japan. We're no longer surprised to see QC circles forming in sales organizations that are connected to manufacturers, but now circles are also being formed in appliance stores, bookstores, supermarkets, and department stores, large and small. We even find circles in the service sector — in restaurants, hotels, traditional inns, and golf courses. In financial institutions, QC circles are spreading from large city banks to regional banks and credit unions. The same is true in the insurance industry and the distribution industry — from transport companies to wholesalers. The Japanese construction industry is set up differently. Often, a construction site is a meeting place for diverse types of workers who will not see each other again once the building is finished. But even there, QC circles are alive and well, and a lot of thought goes into making them work.

Presentations at the many QC circle conferences give a clear indication of the variety of industries using them. Indeed, they are not limited to a particular type of enterprise. Some obstacles exist, however. While the manufacturing sector has accumulated know-how through its experiences in many different workplaces, other sectors do not have this level of experience and there may not be enough capable people within a company to lead QC circle activities in its different sectors.

Yet these problems can be solved with experience over time. Every company and industrial sector has its own characteristics and difficulties and only by taking such problems into account can a QC program really develop. For example, company A may be buying the same equipment as company B in the hope of catching up with its competitor's technology. Using the same equipment, however, company B continues to make one improvement after another, and A never catches up. It is no different when companies import QC.

I have said that QC circles are not limited to certain companies; they all rely on good management, however. QC circle activities will not succeed if top management does not support them enthusiastically.

Techniques Are Important

Systems have been created to gather workers' ideas for improvement, including the time-honored suggestion (*teian*) system. Many improvement activities are characterized by the kind of control applied to the particular operation.

When viewed against these other systems and activities, QC circles are characterized by their insistence on probing for causes with the aid of data collected in the workplace and their step-by-step application of statistical quality control techniques. This prevents mistakes in judgment from occurring easily.

A set of elementary techniques known as the seven QC tools for the workplace involves calculations and the drawing of graphs. These seven tools can be mastered by virtually anyone. QC circle activities have been successful because these basic techniques are so easily understood and break down into concrete steps for dealing with particular problems.

It is important to master these techniques. Once this has been done, even less experienced workers can propose improvement plans persuasively and present their conclusions confidently in front of college-trained specialists. Unlike temporary solutions based on intuition, conclusions reached through systematic, thoughtful QC circle deliberations are long-lasting.

It is not enough for top management to order workers to establish QC circles and activities because it wants to introduce quality control throughout the company. The activities might be called quality control, but in reality the company might be instituting something entirely different. All participants must be trained in data collection and use and other basic techniques; this education should be ongoing during all QC circle activities.

An employee participating in a QC circle or tackling problems in the workplace acquires all the skills and techniques he will ever need. Some groups study industrial engineering methods and operations research in addition to normal QC techniques in their circles. Frequently now, we encounter presentations based on these various methods.

Changing Our Perceptions

The system of so-called "scientific management" begun by Taylor and Gilbreth, combined with Henry Ford's successful use of conveyors, robbed workers of the joy of working. "Modern" workers came to see themselves as impersonal cogs in a big organization, chased after by machines to do their bidding. There was no joy in working, no sense that their work might please customers. This world was aptly portrayed by Charlie Chaplin in his film *Modern Times.*

People in QC circles do not feel like insignificant cogs in an organization. They have confidence in what they are doing and feel responsible for their work. By studying the data, they know the significance of their work and understand what will happen if they fail in what they do.

Most Japanese QC circle activities do not take place during regular working hours. Meetings may be held during a lunch break in the form of a round-table discussion or after work. Members bring problems to the meeting and discuss ways of reducing the number of defective units.

In Japan, it has been the custom for many workers to meet at the corner bar or a *pachinko* parlor after work to socialize. QC has changed their lifestyle by giving them something meaningful to do after work. People who had avoided studying, even with overtime pay, found QC easier to study and understand because problems were selected from their immediate environment.

Companies, of course, must provide places for meeting and study. But their support cannot stop there. They must create an atmosphere in which the success of QC is appropriately recognized.

As Japanese companies began to establish factories in the United States, some Japanese questioned the quality of American workers' performance. But Americans are not so different from the Japanese; when their perceptions change, results will also change dramatically.

Quite a few successes have already been achieved in America through the introduction of QC. Many American factories using QC are as efficient as those in Japan and consultants in QC circle activities are prospering.

The influence of the QC circle is gradually increasing, not only in North America, but also in Europe, Central and South America, and Southeast Asia.

Subtle Differences in QC Circles

The concept of the QC circle is now well-known in the industrialized nations. That is very good, but some things are not sufficiently understood. Some people ask: "Isn't Japan's QC circle actually an import from America?" QC is a "small group activity," they say, where people meet to discuss and make suggestions for improvement — something Americans have been doing for a long time.

As I explained earlier, however, the QC circle has established methods and operating procedures. This is one of the basic differences between the Japanese QC circle and America's "small-group" activities, and it is necessary to emphasize it.

Data are indispensable in QC circle activities. If they are the exclusive possession of a small number of managers and staff, however, no matter how hard QC circle members study, and no matter how thoroughly they master their QC methods, they cannot make effective use of their skills.

In fact, QC circle activity *begins* with the sharing of data with circle members, and that is what leads to their active, willing involvement. To suggest that such activity takes work away from staff or management could not be farther from the truth.

But we cannot teach the methods, provide the data, and then just say "start" — although technically speaking, that is all that is expected. Such an approach fails to recognize the fundamental differences between the QC circle and all other small-group activities. Failure to understand the essence of the QC circle may contribute to the notion that it is no different than the typical American small group.

The central issue is what is in the minds of QC circle members. We can use words like "volition" and "consciousness," but the fact that members really *feel like doing the work* makes the difference. This is not the sort of thing that can be achieved by surface incentives such as a bonus or overtime pay.

Subordinates are always very perceptive when it comes to observing the attitudes of their superiors. If superiors do not show a true commitment to QC, subordinates may still agree politely when told to undertake QC. In their hearts, however, they will know that the campaign is only a passing phase. Unless top management recognizes its responsibility for making QC a success, failure is inevitable.

Do not jump to the conclusion that this rule applies only to Japanese businesses. In both Eastern and Western companies, we need enthusiastic support from top management, a company philosophy that provides definite goals, and a *shafu* that respects these things. We need concern for customers and the realization that such concern is the true basis of manufacturing. We need a sense of mission, a sense that without the efforts each of us undertakes, quality cannot be improved or even maintained. We also need a sense of solidarity and a shared joy of accomplishment. All of these factors can influence perception and the willingness of QC circle members to participate fully in circle activities.

CHAPTER | 11

Peripheral Topics

True Intention *(Honne)* and Stated Reason *(Tatemae)*

These days there is a lot of talk in Japan about issues created by our public policy, that is, the justifications or reasons for our actions that we are willing to state publicly (*tatemae*). Whenever we discuss something, the issue of stated reason versus true intention or motive (*honne*) surfaces almost immediately. On the basis of *tatemae*, something previously agreed upon may suddenly be scrapped. For example, for the sake of *tatemae* many nuclear powered ships are still docked. We built a international airport in Narita, but for the sake of *tatemae*, many years went by before airplanes ever flew from it. We all know that transportation supports industrial activities and is one of the moving forces in creating wealth. An argument based on public outward policy, however, prevents even new jet planes, which are relatively free of noise pollution, from landing at certain airports.

Specialists on quality control consider the degree of contribution an important concept. In other words, we start from larger issues and leave minor points to the last — this is what has made us successful. People who talk about *tatemae* in manufacturing, however, do not appreciate the concept of degree of contribution. In fact, for the sake of policy, they may even disregard proof provided by the facts (data). In quality control everything must be carried out in terms of our intentions, *honne*, on the basis of objective reality. In quality control we deal with facts and cannot say such things as "In principle, . . ." We must call a spade a spade. No matter how convincing a theory, if in reality it produces tons of defective products, it is useless to us.

Yet in factories, many people still insist on bringing in *tatemae*, especially those who like theoretical arguments. There are the data, but instead of relying on them, someone will always insist on quoting a famous person and explaining the situation in eloquent terms. So far so good; but when questions about the next step surface, such people have nothing to contribute. If we persuade them to develop improvement plans and apply them, we find in most instances that their plans don't work. A factory is a place where we make things — it is not a forum in which to debate doctrines.

From this perspective, quality control belongs to the school of positivism. Nowadays, international conferences on quality control are held frequently. At these meetings, the Japanese always speak with *honne* and insist on providing corroborative evidence. In contrast, those countries where quality control is not well developed make abstract presentations; in fact, the less developed a country, the more abstract the presentation. They appear sound, and as they explain their theories, we cannot help but be impressed. But when we ask a simple question like, "What is the actual condition of your factory?" we seldom receive an answer. Japanese presentations, on the other hand, are usually down to earth and backed by data. Once the question and answer period begins, questions never seem to end.

As I watch these intense exchanges I realize how firmly Japan's form of quality control has taken root in Japan. And I also realize the enormous effort it will take to achieve the same level of involvement in other countries.

Traditionally, people in Japan dedicated their lives to make their *honne* and *tatemae* consistent. Discrepancies between the two caused some samurai to commit suicide through the act of *seppuku*. If we find any discrepancy between our principles and what we actually do, then we must re-examine our principles.

Automation and QC

There was a time when people would say, without much re-flection, that once automation took hold in a company, QC would become obsolete. This is another unrealistic point of view. Mechanization, specialization, and management each perform distinct functions. No one with any experience in management would ever think that automation would elimi-nate the need for QC.

Unless the defect rate has already been reduced significantly, the introduction of automated equipment, no matter how new, will not be successful. Surprisingly, this fact is not yet common knowledge. The indiscriminate introduction of automated machines cannot by itself lead to an increase in productivity.

A company that produces a lot of defective units has not yet learned how to produce its own products. When automated machines are introduced under those circumstances, the machines may end up creating mountains of defective units — very efficiently. Of course, the introduction of automated machines has improved conditions in some instances, even when there was no knowledge of QC. With the new machines, process capabilities improved and dispersion decreased. Not knowing why this has happened, however, those companies may still face a crisis in the future. In such cases, the machines are not being fully utilized. Let me give an example to illustrate this point.

A British manufacturer of plate glass machines is the only producer of these machines world-wide. All plate glass makers use this machine. The plate glass made in Japan is of the highest quality, yet inexpensively made. What quality materials are the Japanese makers using? The machine manufacturer decided to send a delegation of observers to Japan. What they discovered was that the Japanese producers generally used lower quality materials but succeeded in making better quality plate glass.

The plate glass machine represented automation at its best. The Japanese simply used it more efficiently. They had the ability to use the machine fully because they had superior man-agement techniques.

Quality control is the ability to produce a product with a desired quality in the manner one wishes. At that point, a company has reached what Shewhart called the controlled state. No matter how new or efficient an automated machine may be, it cannot be used successfully if introduced in a company that has not reached this controlled state.

Middle- and Small-Scale Industries in Times of High Growth

- At a factory that produces "automatic" pencils, automated machines run 24 hours a day. At night there is no one on the factory floor. Three-shift 24-hour operation is considered old-fashioned today; what comes after automation is a factory without people.

- At a factory producing printed circuits, personnel was reduced from 280 to 23 through automation. Of course, the factory operates 24 hours a day. Interestingly, neither of these factories is owned by a large corporation.

- "Why did you decide to make such a large investment in equipment?" I asked at one of these companies. The youthful director of its technical division explained: "In a period of rapid economic growth, a shortage of workers almost forced us to shut down the factory. Workers are going to large corporations; they don't want to work for smaller companies like ours. Without this new equipment, we would not have survived."

We tend to think of small- and medium-size companies as backward factories with shabby facilities and low productivity. Among the companies that received their baptism by fire during the oil crisis are quite a few smaller companies many of whom have more fully automated factories than larger industries. If, after visiting such a factory, you visit one of the larger corporations, you will immediately notice the greater number of workers per square foot in the latter.

As I see it, the rapid growth of the economy pushed small- and middle-size companies toward modernization even harder than it pushed the large ones. The companies that succeeded have some of the best management systems.

Illustrated in the form of a flow chart, it looks like this:

Rapid economic growth → Expanding demand → Shortage of personnel → Automation → Repayment of debt → Oil crisis → Period of selectivity and restructuring → High income

In other words, the cost of facilities acquired to institute automation was quickly recouped because of rapid economic growth. In fact, many of these facilities were almost fully paid for by the time the recession came.

For the large companies that had added personnel somewhat thoughtlessly during the period of high growth, recession was a time of reckoning. They had to cut back on personnel in whatever way they could when the oil crisis hit. By comparison, middle- and small-size enterprises that had introduced automation and developed excellent management systems fared quite well. They were capable of using the new machines fully. Their conversion to automation succeeded because quality control was conducted thoroughly and their processes were in the controlled state. Had they been introduced under any other circumstances, these automated machines would be at best a useless treasure to their owners and at worst the cause of bankruptcy.

A company's size has nothing to do with its ability to engage in quality control. Many companies with small buildings and unpretentious factories conduct quality control superbly. In my opinion, these are also the companies that will successfully introduce the latest in automation.

If We Could Determine Costs Only by Weight...

Let us consider what determines the cost of a product. Essentially, the raw materials we use to produce things are available to us free of charge — the treasures the earth prepares for us lie buried, waiting to be taken. We may need to pay a premium for mining rights, but that is not a major consideration. The first real expense is the mining, but it is surprisingly inexpensive — we dig a hole in the ground and put a stick of dynamite in it. We get several tons of unprocessed minerals or ore in this way, haul it to the sea by truck, and ship it. For example, iron ore for Japan usually comes from Australia and North America. Each ton costs about ¥3,000 or $15.00 (in 1985). Together with coke and limestone, the ore is heated in a furnace to make pig iron. Steel is made by purifying melted pig iron in a converter where carbon and other impurities are removed. The steel is formed into plate or bar and sent to our factory. We cut, bend, polish, and prepare the surface and assemble it into appliances. If at final inspection one of those appliances is declared unacceptable, all previous efforts will have been wasted.

Generally speaking, cost competition is determined by yield. Most factories have similar facilities for production of a particular item, and the cost of personnel does not differ significantly between employers. So in fierce competition, the deciding factor is the rate of yield.

Once it seemed like a good idea to move factories to developing countries to take advantage of lower wages. In many instances, however, the actual cost was higher than anticipated. The main reasons for this were higher defect rates and lower productivity.

When the defect rate goes down significantly, the cost of processing becomes less significant. The differences can be measured in terms of materials costs. In the final analysis, cost is proportionate to the weight of the materials, the only real variable when all other factors are under control. It follows that real success lies in being able to know the cost through the weight.

We can talk about the level of processing, but there are limits to such a discussion. The semiconductor industry is a good example of this. The large-scale integrated circuit (LSI) that contains thousands of transistors initially cost about ¥ 30,000 (approximately $150). However, in terms of material, it con-sists of a single silicon chip about 3 square millimeters in size. It now costs less than ¥ 500 ($2.50). This cost reduction was achieved through increased yield alone. It's amazing to think that several thousand transistors can be bought for around $2.00 — one transistor does not even cost a penny! It is true that the LSI contains thousands of transistors, but looking only at the material, it's just a silicon chip. $2.50 is probably still too much to charge for it. This is the secret of industrial power.

Continuous Improvement

Foreigners visiting Japanese factories cannot always see how well the Japanese are actually doing because they cannot see the continuous process of improvement.

For example, an automobile manufacturer bought a 3,000 ton stamping machine from West Germany. Once put together, it was a massive machine. Its production capacity was enorm-ous, as was the work needed to change its die. The entire changeover process took eight hours, a full working day, so there was no choice but to change the die on Sunday. Stamping began again the following day, making either the right or left door. However, in manufacturing automobiles, having doors for only one side does little good. The following Sunday, the die had to be changed again to make the doors for the other side. The stamping machine was highly efficient, but it created mountains of work-in-progress. To house this inventory, a big warehouse became necessary.

The auto maker started to think about shortening the setup for the die as a way to solve his problem. After much work, setup time was reduced from eight hours to seven, to six, and to five; now it takes only 20 minutes. Changing the die daily, whenever necessary, eliminated both the work-in-progress inven-tory and the need for a warehouse and drastically reduced costs.

At this stage, a representative of the West German stamping machine manufacturer came to visit. When informed that the exchange of die took only 20 minutes, the visitor flatly refused to believe it.

Improvement at the company had gone far beyond anyone's expectations. That, in essence, is the strength of Japanese industry. A casual observer, however, sees only the stamping machine producing doors or other parts, and cannot appreciate the full impact of continuous improvement behind that simple activity.

How *could* the exchange of die be reduced so dramatically?

The company used a cause-and-effect diagram to analyze the situation. When the machine was first purchased, a crane had been brought in to hoist the die during changeovers. But there were only two cranes in the entire factory, and if a die was being changed in one location, workers ready for changeover in another location had to wait. To hoist the die, however, it was not really necessary to use the crane. When workers switched to forklifts, all dies could be changed at once. This improvement alone saved a substantial amount of time.

Nuts had to be loosened and removed to change from one die to the other and then replaced and tightened again. Workers studying this part of the changeover operation were troubled by the amount of time it took to bring wrenches to the site to remove the nuts. If wrenches had to be brought in, they reasoned, why not attach them directly to the nuts? So the workers simply welded wrenches to the nuts. When the time came to remove the die, each worker grasped a wrench, and with a shout of "*yoisho*" ("heave-ho!") removed all the nuts. These are the kinds of improvements that helped reduce the changeover time to 20 minutes.

Continuous improvement, even though facilities and equipment remain the same, is one of the secrets of Japan's industrial success.

Invisible Improvement

Unlike new machines, improvements made through better management are invisible, and uninformed people often miss them. For example, a casual driver may not know that road congestion has been reduced by staggering lights. Before the improvement, car travel was a lot of stop and go. Afterwards, drivers may notice only that the trip is smoother, nothing more.

Similarly, people visiting factories do not understand what they are seeing. This lack of understanding is not confined to foreigners or to the case of the 3,000 ton stamping machine. For example, in a steel mill, pig iron is heated in a converter and oxygen blasted in from the top to blow away carbon impurities and produce steel. If too much carbon is blown away, however, the finished product will be too soft. To create the desired hardness in steel, the process must be halted when the carbon is at a certain percentage level. This is very difficult. Normally, the process takes 15 to 16 minutes, but the success rate on the first try is only about 60 percent. If the first try is unsuccessful, samples are taken to determine the level of carbon content. If it is too low, carbon will have to be added to the entire batch.

In one particular steel mill, the first try success rate is 95 percent. Each converter contains about 600 tons, and since carbon seldom needs to be added to the entire batch, the mill's cost is substantially lower than that of other mills.

Converters are the same everywhere with the same equipment, but at this mill the method of use is much more efficient.

Though invisible to the eye, cost reduction has had an enormous impact on the industry. It is due to this improvement alone that the price of steel in Japan only doubled during the seventies in the midst of skyrocketing energy and materials costs.

Companies throughout Japan are continuously engaged in this type of invisible improvement activities. The speed with which they are able to complete one process of change and move on to the next stage is unmatched in other countries and further contributes to Japan's industrial competitiveness.

CHAPTER | 12

Epilogue

Distortion in the Japanese Economy

The oil crises of the 1970s were the catalysts that forced modernization of Japanese industries. Up until that time, the high growth rate had sustained the economy. Despite inefficiencies, industries could increase their sales and continue to grow. The first oil crisis forced these industries to improve their basic structure, and they became "lean and mean" as a result. Due to this strengthening of their corporate characteristics, they were able to withstand the shock of the second oil crisis. was able to weather them as well as Japan. Some countries were hit so hard by these waves of economic change that they have not yet recovered. Others, though less badly affected, could not maintain the level of economic stability they had worked so hard to achieve.

The degree to which different countries were affected economically by the oil crises has been a cause of friction between them. Naturally, Japan's future economic growth has also been affected deeply.

One of the most significant examples is the friction between Japan and the United States. Historically, the United States had always been the premier producer of automobiles. As recently as a decade ago, no one would have thought that Japan could become the challenger it is today. Japan is also making an impressive inroad into the world market share in the machine-tool industry.

The prediction of a golden age of Japanese industry was almost fulfilled in the early 1980s. Some dark valleys still remain, however, and have begun to manifest as a distortion in prices.

I recall an incident in 1980, at an international conference in Tokyo. One of the most popular souvenir items sought by foreign participants was a pocket calculator. A participant asked me to buy him one and I was able to get it for under $10. An American participant saw it and remarked: "We can buy four pocket calculators for the price of one dinner at this hotel. What is the reason for these inequities?"

The greatest problem the Japanese economy must face today is the imbalance in prices. Some of our products are the cheapest in the world, but others are the most expensive (beef, for example). Most of our industrial products belong in the first category, while food and services belong in the second. This distortion has reached a point where it can no longer be tolerated.

There is one clear way of fixing this distortion and that is to improve those sectors where productivity still lags behind.

Technology Transfer

If we can transfer our know-how in industrial fields where we have the highest productivity to sectors where our productivity is low, we will be able to resolve this economic distortion.

The term "technology transfer" means taking technology from one field and applying it in another. If we can succeed in this, the Japanese economy can experience even more growth.

It is common knowledge among manufacturers that adhering to the three Ss can result in higher productivity. The three Ss are: *standardization, simplification,* and *specialization.* What follows is an example of how these principles have been transferred to a sector that is known for its low productivity.

Yoshinoya is a fast food chain selling bowls of rice and beef. Although lately it has experienced some setbacks, Yoshinoya owes its initial success to strict adherence to the principle of the three Ss. It has proven to the public that even in Japan where food prices are very high, a restaurant can provide a nutritious meal for only $1.50. It has also succeeded in raising its ratio of operation for equipment and facilities to customers served, by reducing the time customers must wait for their meals.

In short, this restaurant has succeeded in raising the productivity of a service sector industry by transferring to that sector expertise that has proven effective in the industrial sector.

Today we are experiencing diversity of customer demands. Auto makers can provide cars that fit customer specifications, following what is known in Japan as the "order entry" system. Customers do not have to accept the colors and models chosen by manufacturers. Instead, they can obtain any combination offered in the company catalogue. These orders are entered on a computer connected to the production line and cars are finished in accordance with them. With this ordering system, manufacturers can even promise delivery of a car by a certain day.

Development and spread of computers have made this type of purchasing possible. With the fantastic increase in the use of personal computers, personalized selection of products will soon spread to all areas of the economy. In other words, we may still mass produce, but we will be able to provide "made to order" products for all customers.

Toward the 1990s

In 1980, when I spoke about Japan's high productivity at the conference on semiconductors in the United States, a congressman made the following comment at the reception: "I understand what you are saying, but to raise productivity we have to invest more. The high rate of interest prevents us from doing it."

I asked him, "Do we really need money to raise productivity? I know some methods call for heavier investments, but there are many ways to raise productivity and not spend a penny."

The congressman was puzzled by my answer. "When you drive," I said, "you may have to stop at every corner because of the traffic lights. But if you stagger lights to turn green with the flow of the traffic, cars can proceed without stopping, and travel time is cut in half. Productivity would be raised 100 percent, and only a slight adjustment in the timing of the traffic lights would be required."

The congressman caught on quickly: "In other words," he said, "you want to solve these problems with software!"

Well said! As I mentioned earlier, quality control is one of our "soft" techniques. We can raise productivity by introducing large machines, but it will definitely require additional funds. Most people are limited to these methods in their thinking. However, we can also obtain a significant increase in productivity by changing our way of "driving," that is, the way people and machines work together. QC is one such technique.

As we look forward to the year 2000, we must accept the task of improving every area where productivity is still low. Many of these problems can be solved with our "soft" technology. This will help us reduce the absurd distortions we face in our present structure.

QC is a tool for improvement. Today, in your own company, there is certainly a division or section with low productivity. Search for problems there and develop methods to make improvements. In doing so, you will also be helping others within your industry and in your country become more productive.

About the Author

H ajime Karatsu was born in Hyogo Prefecture, Japan, in 1919. He graduated in 1942 from the Imperial University of Tokyo with a degree in electrical engineering. In 1948 he entered Nippon Telegraph and Telephone Public Corporation. He joined Matsushita Communication Industrial Co., Ltd., in 1961, advancing to director in 1971 and managing director in 1978. In 1984 he became a technical advisor to Matsushita Electric Industrial Co., Ltd., and in 1986 he joined the faculty of Tokai University's R & D Institute. Mr. Karatsu received a Deming Prize in 1981 for his work in quality control and was honored by the Ministry of Education in 1984 for his distinguished contributions to the development of industrial education in Japan. This is his first book to be published in English.

Index

123

Other Books on
Quality Improvement

Productivity Press publishes and distributes materials on productivity, quality improvement, and employee involvement for business and industry, academia, and the general market. Many products are direct source materials from Japan that have been translated into English for the first time and are available exclusively from Productivity. Supplemental services include conferences, seminars, in-house training programs, and industrial study missions. Send for free book catalog.

Management for Quality Improvement
The 7 New QC Tools
edited by Shigeru Mizuno

Building on the traditional seven QC tools, these new tools were developed specifically for managers. They help in planning, troubleshooting, and communicating with maximum effectiveness at every stage of a quality improvement program. Only recently made available in the U.S., they are certain to advance quality improvement efforts for anyone involved in project management, quality assurance, MIS, or TQC.
ISBN 0-915299-29-1 / 318 pages / $59.95

Canon Production System
Creative Involvement of the Total Workforce
compiled by the Japan Management Association

A fantastic success story! Canon set a goal to increase productivity by three percent per month — and achieved it! The first book-length case study to show how to combine the most effective Japanese management principles and quality improvement techniques into one overall strategy that improves every area of the company on a continual basis. Shows how the seven new QC tools are applied in a matrix management model.
ISBN 0-915299-06-2 / 232 pages / $36.95

Workplace Management
by Taiichi Ohno

An in-depth view of how one of this century's leading industrial thinkers approaches problem solving and continuous improvement. Gleaned from Ohno's 40 years of experimentation and innovation at Toyota Motor Co., where he created JIT, this book explains the concepts that Ohno considers to be most important to successful management, with an emphasis on quality.
ISBN 0-915299-19-4 / 166 pages / $34.95

Productivity Press, Dept. BK, P.O. Box 3007, Cambridge, MA 02140 (617) 497-5146

Non-Stock Production
The Shingo System for Continuous Improvement
by Shigeo Shingo

Shingo, who helped develop JIT at Toyota with Taiichi Ohno, teaches how to implement non-stock production in your JIT manufacturing operations. The culmination of his extensive writings on efficient production management and continuous improvement, his latest book is an essential companion volume to his other books on key elements of JIT, and gives the most comprehensive understanding available anywhere on quality in the production function.
ISBN 0-915299-30-5 / 480 pages / $75.00

Zero Quality Control
Source Inspection and the Poka-yoke System
by Shigeo Shingo, translated by Andrew P. Dillon

A remarkable combination of source inspection and mistake-proofing devices (to detect errors before they become defects) eliminates the need for statistical quality control. Shingo shows how this proven system for reducing defects to zero turns out the highest quality products in the shortest period of time. With over 100 specific examples illustrated. (Audio-visual training program also available.)
ISBN 0-915299-07-0 / 305 pages / $65.00

Managerial Engineering
Techniques for Improving Quality and Productivity in the Workplace
by Ryuji Fukuda

A proven path to managerial success, based on reliable methods developed by one of Japan's leading productivity experts and winner of the coveted Deming Prize for quality. Dr. W. Edwards Deming, world-famous consultant on quality, says that the book "provides an excellent and clear description of the devotion and methods of Japanese management to continual improvement of quality." (CEDAC training programs also available.)
ISBN 0-915299-09-7 / 179 pages / $34.95

BOOKS AVAILABLE FROM PRODUCTIVITY PRESS

Christopher, William F. **Productivity Measurement Handbook**
ISBN 0-915299-05-4 / 1983 / 680 pages / looseleaf / $137.95

Fukuda, Ryuji. **Managerial Engineering: Techniques for Improving Quality and Productivity in the Workplace**
ISBN 0-915299-09-7 / 1984 / 206 pages / hardcover / $34.95

Hatakeyama, Yoshio. **Manager Revolution! A Guide to Survival in Today's Changing Workplace**
ISBN 0-915299-10-0 / 1984 / 198 pages / hardcover / $24.95

Japan Management Association and Constance E. Dyer. **Canon Production System: Creative Involvement of the Total Workforce**
ISBN 0-915299-06-2 / 1987 / 251 pages / hardcover / $36.95

Japan Management Association. **Kanban and Just-In-Time at Toyota: Management Begins at the Workplace,** *translated by David J. Lu*
ISBN 0-915299-08-9 / 1986 / 186 pages / hardcover / $29.95

Lu, David J. **Inside Corporate Japan: The Art of Fumble-Free Management**
ISBN 0-915299-16-X / 1987 / 278 pages / hardcover / $24.95

Ohno, Taiichi. **Toyota Production System: Beyond Large-Scale Production**
ISBN 0-915299-14-3 / 1988 / 176 pages / hardcover / $39.95

Ohno, Taiichi. **Workplace Management**
ISBN 0-915299-19-4 / 1988 / 176 pages / hardcover / $34.95

Shingo, Shigeo. **A Revolution in Manufacturing: The SMED System,** *translated by Andrew P. Dillon*
ISBN 0-915299-03-8 / 1985 / 383 pages / hardcover / $65.00

Shingo, Shigeo. **Zero Quality Control: Source Inspection and the Poka-Yoke System,** *translated by Andrew P. Dillon*
ISBN 0-915299-07-0 / 1986 / 328 pages / hardcover / $65.00

Shingo, Shigeo. **The Sayings of Shigeo Shingo: Key Strategies for Plant Improvement,** *translated by Andrew P. Dillon*
ISBN 0-915299-15-1 / 1987 / 207 pages / hardcover / $36.95

AUDIO-VISUAL PROGRAMS

Shingo, Shigeo. **The SMED System,** *translated by Andrew P. Dillon*
ISBN 0-915299-11-9 / slides / $749.00
ISBN 0-915299-27-5 / video / $749.00

Shingo, Shigeo. **The Poka-Yoke System,** *translated by Andrew P. Dillon*
ISBN 0-915299-13-5 / slides / $749.00
ISBN 0-915299-28-3 / video / $749.00

Productivity Press, Dept. BK, P.O. Box 3007, Cambridge, MA 02140 (617) 497-5146

SPRING/SUMMER BOOKS FROM PRODUCTIVITY PRESS

Ford, Henry. **Today and Tomorrow** (originally published 1926)
ISBN 0-915299-36-4 / June 1988 / $24.95

Karatsu, Hajime. **TQC Wisdom of Japan: Managing for Total Quality Control**
ISBN 0-915299-18-6 / June 1988 / $34.95

Karatsu, Hajime. **Tough Words for American Industry**
ISBN 0-915299-25-9 / May 1988 / $24.95

Mizuno, Shigeru (ed.) **Management for Quality Improvement:
The 7 New QC Tools**
ISBN 0-915299-29-1 / June 1988 / $59.95

Ohno, Taiichi and Setsuo Mito. **Just-In-Time for Today and Tomorrow:
A Total Management System**
ISBN 0-915299-20-8 / August 1988 / $34.95

Shingo, Shigeo. **Non-Stock Production: The Shingo System for
Continuous Improvement**
ISBN 0-915299-30-5 / June 1988 / $75.00

Shinohara, Isao (ed.) **New Production System: JIT — Crossing Industry
Boundaries**
ISBN 0-915299-21-6 / May 1988 / $34.95

TO ORDER: Write, phone or fax Productivity Press, Dept. BK, P.O. Box 3007, Cambridge, MA 02140, phone 617/497-5146, fax 617/868-3524. Send check or charge to your credit card (American Express, Visa, MasterCard accepted). Include street address for UPS delivery.

U.S. ORDERS: Add $3 shipping for first book, $1 each additional. CT residents add 7.5% and MA residents 5% sales tax. Add $5 for each AV.

FOREIGN ORDERS: Payment must be made in U.S. dollars. For Canadian orders, add $8 shipping for first book, $2 each additional. Orders to other countries are on a proforma basis; please indicate shipping method desired.

NOTE: Prices subject to change without notice.

Productivity Press, Dept. BK, P.O. Box 3007, Cambridge, MA 02140 (617) 497-5146